SUMMARY

Since 1993 at the latest, when Andrew W. Marshall and his Office of Net Assessment in the Office of the Secretary of Defense (OSD) introduced into public debate the concept of a Revolution in Military affairs (RMA), the idea of revolutionary change in warfare has gripped the official U.S. strategic imagination. All such master notions, or meta narratives, have lengthy antecedents. The provenance of RMA can be traced in the use of laser-guided bombs in Vietnam; in the 1970s "Assault Breaker" project to develop rocket-delivered smart bomblets to target Soviet armor far behind the front; in Soviet speculation about a Military-Technical Revolution (MTR) and the feasibility of "reconnaissance-strike complexes"; in the *Discriminate Deterrence* reports of the late 1980s (sponsored by then Under Secretary of Defense for Policy, Dr. Fred Ikle, and inspired by Dr. Albert Wohlstetter); by the dramatic effects of stealth and precision in the Gulf War of 1991; and, "off piste" as it were, by a rising argument among academic historians of early-modern Europe.

U.S. debate evolved into official commitment. RMA was to be realized as transformation or, for a scarcely less ambitious expression, as revolutionary change in the way American forces would fight. The fascination with revolutionary change persisted through the 1990s, survived, indeed was given "gravity assists" by the newly mandated *Quadrennial Defense Reviews* (QDRs), by a change in administration in 2001, and was scarcely dented as the dominant defense concept by September 11, 2001 (9/11). Truly it seems to be a big idea for all seasons: for the no-name post-Cold War decade, now for the Age of Terror, and prospectively for whatever the decades ahead will bring.

This monograph provides an audit, a not-unfriendly critical review, of the concept of revolutionary military change. It offers a review of what those who theorize about, and those who are committed by policy to execute, such a revolution ought to know about their subject. As the subtitle of the analysis announces, the leading edge of the argument is the potency, indeed the sovereign importance, of warfare's contexts.

The monograph strives to clarify the confusion over definitions. It points out that the concept of RMA, though less so the even grander idea of military revolution (MR), is eminently and irreducibly contestable. The RMA debate has provided a happy hunting ground for academic historians to wage protracted internecine combat. All definitions of RMA present problems, a fact which is of some practical consequence for a U.S. military now firmly taking what is intended to be a revolutionary path. This author prefers a truly minimalist definition: an RMA is a radical change in the conduct and character of war. The more detail one adds to the definition, the more hostages are offered to reasonable objection.

The first of the three major sections poses and answers the most basic of questions, the ones that really matter most, about revolutionary change in warfare. It asks: Does the RMA concept make sense? Is it useful? Does it much matter? Is not military change more a product of evolution than revolution? Are not continuities at least as important as changes in their relative contribution to military effectiveness? And, is revolutionary change the high road to victory? By and large, though not without some rough handling, the RMA concept, the notion of transformation, or simply the descriptive idea of revolutionary change, survive the ordeal of question and answer.

The second major section, the heart of the monograph, seeks to advance understanding of revolutionary change in warfare, the core purpose of this enterprise, by explaining that war (and its conduct in warfare) is dominated by, indeed what it really is all about—its contexts. To the best of this author's knowledge, to date no other analysis has taken such a holistic view of warfare's contexts with reference to RMA. This analysis breaks new ground. The thesis here is that context provides the key to recognizing and understanding revolutionary change in warfare. The argument is presented through the explanation of the significance of six contexts: the political, the strategic, the social-cultural, the economic, the technological, and the geographical. While each context is vitally significant, the occurrence of war, as well as its course in warfare, its outcome, and its consequences, derive their meaning only from politics. As this author argued in a recent monograph for the Strategic Studies Institute, *Transformation and Strategic Surprise*, American strategic performance is apt to disappoint on occasions because the strategic bridge between military behavior and the political context is not always in good enough repair.

The concluding, yet substantial, section assembles the arguments and insights from the previous discussions into seven broad findings, and it draws out the implications of each for the U.S. Armed Forces in general, and the Army in particular. The seven findings are effectively self-explanatory.

1. Contexts rule!

2. Revolutionary change in warfare may be less important than revolutionary change in social attitudes to war and the military.

3. Historical research shows that there are vital conditions for success in carrying through revolutionary changes in warfare.

4. Recognition of change in warfare is one thing, but understanding the character, relevance, and implications of change is something else entirely, given the sovereignty of the political and strategic contexts.

5. When we effect a revolutionary change in the way we fight, we must do so adaptably and flexibly. If we fail the adaptability test, we are begging to be caught out by the diversity and complexity of future warfare. If we lock ourselves into a way of war that is highly potent only across a narrow range of strategic and military contexts, and hence operational taskings, we will wound our ability to recognize and understand other varieties of radical change in warfare. Moreover, we will be slow, if able at all in a relevant time span, to respond effectively to them.

6. Revolutionary change in warfare always triggers a search for antidotes. Eventually the antidotes triumph. They can take any or all of tactical, operational, strategic, or political forms. The solution, in principle if not always in practice, is to carry through an RMA that is adaptable, flexible, and dynamic as recommended in 5. above.

7. Revolutionary change in warfare is only revealed by the "audit of war," and not necessarily reliably even then. And if it is to be conducted competently, review of that audit must take full account of war's complex nature.

RECOGNIZING AND UNDERSTANDING REVOLUTIONARY CHANGE IN WARFARE: THE SOVEREIGNTY OF CONTEXT

War is more than a true chameleon that slightly adapts its characteristics to the given case. As a total phenomenon its dominant tendencies always make war a remarkable trinity—composed of primordial violence, hatred, and enmity, which are to be regarded as a blind natural force; of the play of chance and probability within which the creative spirit is free to roam; and of its element of subordination, as an instrument of policy, which makes it subject to reason alone.

Clausewitz, 1832[1]

[A]ll wars are things of the *same* nature . . .

Clausewitz, 1832[2]

[T]he only empirical data we have about how people conduct war and behave under its stresses is our experience with it in the past, however much we have to make adjustments for subsequent changes in conditions.

Bernard Brodie, 1976[3]

Introduction.

It is 12 years since Andrew W. Marshall lent his formidable personal authority, as well as the weight of his small but influential Office of Net Assessment in the Office of the Secretary of Defense (OSD), to the proposition that a revolution in military affairs (RMA) might or could be underway.[4] The history of the "great RMA debate" of the 1990s and beyond remains to be written, though preferably, one hopes, not until many more years have elapsed. At present the story is unduly incomplete, and too many commentator-historians would find themselves employing their versions of recent history in the service of contemporary argument. That granted, national security policy, grand strategy, military strategy, doctrine, and force structure cannot be put on hold pending properly scholarly assay. As war is conducted in a climate of uncertainty, so those who aspire to offer strategic advice must do their best with imperfect information and the unavoidable biases bequeathed by the time and place of their writing.

The purpose of this monograph is to provide answers to the questions that are both explicit and implicit in its title. The analysis can be viewed as an assessment of the RMA debate at the 12-year mark by a participant-observer.[5] It is not, however, primarily an exercise in history. It is, rather, an attempt to corral and make intelligible for potential use by policymakers and military professionals, "findings" from the years of often heated debate on RMA. Strategic knowledge needs to be useful knowledge. It is in the very nature and purpose of strategic studies for it to be a pragmatic enterprise.

For every fashionable concept there is a season, and inevitably so it has proved for RMA. However, the RMA concept has demonstrated an exceptional potency and longevity, facts plainly attributable both to the attractions of the promise in the idea and to its strong appeal in American culture. Revolutionary change in warfare is a notion that cannot be dismissed with a yawn. Unlike, say, network-centricity or effects-based operations, revolutionary change is not a cliché that conceals rediscovery of the long familiar and well-appreciated.[6] Whatever one's thoughts about the RMA hypothesis, be they positive or negative on balance, there can be no denying, on the one hand, the appeal of riding the wave of revolutionary change, or, on the other, the fear that one might be the victim of some other polity riding that wave. Now that the RMA debate of the 1990s by and large has matured into argument about the realization of RMA in a lengthy process of "transformation," the follow-on magic concept, what do we think we know about recognizing and understanding revolutionary change in warfare? No less to the point, what are the practical implications of that knowledge for national security, strategy, and defense planning?

The mission of this monograph is to provide some answers to these questions. The trajectory of the analysis proceeds through three sections. The first offers definitions and discusses the most significant theoretical matters. I do this without apology to the historians among my readers. As a controversial British historian, John Vincent, has noted, "historians themselves . . . were never ones for concepts, let alone rigour."[7] That is too sweeping a judgment, but it is true enough to be distinctly relevant to the course of the RMA debate, past and present. The next section, the core of the work, also is somewhat theoretical in that it strives to explain the structure of the subject of warfare with reference to the most vital contexts, albeit without downplaying the vital role of human agency and plain old accident and luck. In its concluding section, the monograph provides a set of "findings and implications" concerning the most important of the challenges posed by revolutionary change in warfare, with a view to separating the dross from the gold. Particular attention is paid to the authoritative roles of warfare's several contexts.

The use of history, or should one say the past, is controversial, but it is the only potential evidence available.[8] If we deny the past, the result has to be analysis and prognosis resting entirely upon current concerns and the nostrums of today. That might be good enough, but it would seem to this theorist to be a gratuitously reckless self-impoverishment.

Revolutionary Change in Warfare: What Are We Talking About?

Often only a fine line separates a necessary precision in language from the malady of scholarly pedantry. Probably most readers of this monograph already are comfortable with the idea of a revolutionary change in warfare. After all, it is an idea blessed by the authority of seemingly endless repetition over the past dozen years, while also it carries an all but self-evident meaning. Revolutionary change is not exactly an obscure, arcane, idea. It is not unreasonable to believe that we can recognize such change when it looms or occurs. To meet the test of common sense, revolutionary change must be change that overturns an existing order. But, is our subject strictly change in warfare, or must it extend to change in war itself? War and warfare are not synonymous. Warfare is dominated by its several major contexts, not the least among them being the institution of war. It is commonplace for war and warfare to be used interchangeably, an error that has great potential to promote misunderstanding. Lest there be any uncertainty on the matter, this analysis holds that warfare is the actual conduct of war, principally in its strategic and military dimensions, which is to say with regard to the threat or use of force. In contrast, war is a political, and sometimes legal, relationship between belligerents. War also is a social institution. Just as revolutionary change in warfare can be triggered by a transformation of war, so the implications of such change are likely to be driven by the broader transformation, possibly to the point where they are substantially offset by extra-military developments. Should anyone harbor any residual uncertainty on the matter, war is a relationship wherein organized violence is carried on by political units against each other for political motives.

Revolutionary change in warfare is a concept that typically trips off the tongue or out of the computer with scant felt need by its employer for detailed explanation. This may be a sensibly relaxed attitude. However, given the mission of this analysis, to help in the recognition and understanding of revolutionary change in warfare, or RMA, we cannot afford to be completely relaxed about the content of our subject. The scholarly pedant in this theorist would like to know, for preference, exactly what is meant by revolutionary change, or, if that is a demand too far, what is the depth and scope of the uncertainty.

RMA as a professional term of art has rather gone out of fashion, but its meaning effectively is identical to the concept of revolutionary change in warfare. There is a subtle distinction between the two, with RMA possibly carrying some theoretical baggage that simple revolutionary change does not, but truly it is a distinction without a significant difference. Notwithstanding its longevity in defense and academic historical discourse, RMA remains a deeply contested concept. Its historical reality is contested, as indeed is just about everything else about it: for example, its content, utility, and significance. Before too many readers discard this text in irritation at the scholastic trend in the discussion, I must insist that this thus far admittedly rather abstract analysis has profound practical implications for U.S. national security as a whole, and for the Army in particular. What we are discussing is nothing less than the prospects for, and the meaning and probable consequences of, the military transformation to which the American defense establishment has firmly committed itself. The Armed Forces have signed on for a revolutionary change in warfare. It is vital that they should recognize and understand just what it is that transformation implies.

This author prefers minimal definitions that avoid arguable descriptive attributes; readers may find more elaborate definitions attractive. My definition holds that an RMA is a radical change in the character or conduct of war.

In an important book published in 2001, historians Williamson Murray and MacGregor Knox drew attention to a significant distinction between military revolutions (MRs) and RMAs. Whereas the latter are chosen happenings, pursued purposefully by states to produce "new ways of destroying their opponents," MRs "brought systemic changes in politics and society. They were uncontrollable, unpredictable, and unforeseeable. And their impact continues."[9] Murray and Knox identified five MRs: the creation of the modern state and its military institutions in the 17th century; the French Revolution; the Industrial Revolution; World War I, which combined the effects of the previous three; and the Nuclear Revolution. To this list, we may wish to add the Information Revolution. The key difference between an MR and its antecedent and subsequent RMAs is that it forecloses on choice. Polities simply have to cope with the contexts it creates as best they can. This MR/RMA distinction has some significance for this analysis, even though my mission, to investigate the recognition and understanding of revolutionary change in warfare, risks obscuring it. The significance is that if, as I believe, the contemporary process of transformation is best understood as a response to an MR, a military revolution, it is not a matter of policy or strategic choice, at least not overall. Of course, in detail it is eminently challengeable.

Probably the most widely used and accepted detailed definition was provided by Andrew F. Krepinevich in an influential article published in 1994. As a close associate of Andrew W. Marshall, the American godfather of the RMA concept, Krepinevich's definition carried unusual weight. He explained RMA thus:

> What is a military revolution? It is what occurs when the application of new technologies into a significant number of military systems combines with innovative operational concepts and organizational adaptation in a way that fundamentally alters the character and conduct of conflict. It does so by producing a dramatic increase — often an order of magnitude or greater — in the combat potential and military effectiveness of armed forces.[10]

By way of a final offering, a RAND study in 1999 tells us that:

An RMA involves a paradigm shift in the nature and conduct of military operations

- which either *renders obsolete or irrelevant* one or more *core competencies* of a dominant player,
- or creates one or more new core competencies, in some new dimension of warfare,
- or both.[11]

The RAND author, Richard O. Hundley, defines his key term, "core competency," as "[a] fundamental ability that provides the foundation for a set of military capabilities."[12] By way of a contemporary example, Hundley cites the "the ability to detect vehicular targets from the air and attack them with precision weapons is today a core competency of the U.S. Air Force."[13]

Hundley's brave and innovative specification of the passing grade for an RMA provides a test that has some merit, but it is one which this author, perhaps ungenerously, judges unduly restrictive and arguable. Jeremy Black's cautionary words in 1995 continue to warrant respect. Professor Black emphasized the subjective nature of RMA as an historical descriptor. He argued that "there are no agreed-upon criteria by which military change, especially qualitative developments, can be measured or, more significantly, revolution discerned."[14] Whether or not one shares Black's skepticism about the historical sense in the RMA concept, he performs a useful service by reminding us of the contestability of many claims by historians and defense analysts for the presence of RMAs.[15] Scholarly debate about RMA has a real-world resonance. After all, the Armed Forces currently are proceeding through the early stages of what will be a lengthy process designed to achieve transformation, a dynamic condition that we can translate fairly as a revolutionary change in the way warfare is waged. The conceptual RMA horse has already left the theory stable and, indeed, has progressed beyond starter's orders into the race itself. Still it is prudent for officials and soldiers to check on the state of the conceptual runners in the scholarly debate. Strategic ideas, albeit in modified form those derived inductively as well as deductively, fuel policy, plans, and military behavior. So, what is the state of the contemporary debate over RMA, or revolutionary change in warfare?

All strategic debates flourish, then wane and die, as the issue in question is intellectually exhausted, or as policy concerns move on, or both. RMA has been atypical in that it continues to attract interesting commentary, even after 12 years of high exposure. This fact is best explained with reference to its inherent potency; its appeal in American strategic and military culture; its official adoption by both Democratic and Republican administrations, as the master concept inspiring, and in a sense licensing, the transformation of the country's armed forces; and, last but not least, to the extensive, if not very intensive, U.S. experience of armed combat from Kosovo in 1999, through Afghanistan in 2001-02, to Iraq in 2003-present. To state the matter directly, the Department of Defense is endeavoring to effect an RMA, a revolutionary change in the way U.S. military forces conduct warfare. For an approximate historical analogy, one has to look back to the 1950s, when the newly minted theory of stable nuclear deterrence gradually was accepted and then was all but embalmed as the intellectual architecture which dominated U.S. defense policy for nearly 40 years. There was, however, at least one vital difference between the theories of deterrence and RMA. The former was driven by the pressing needs of a political context of acute interstate hostility, while the latter is not.[16] Nonetheless, deterrence and RMA share as a common feature the character of being a response to technological challenge, even though the former was shaped by the needs of a very definite political context of threats, while the latter was not. The theory of nuclear deterrence was developed so as to make sense of, and guide policy, strategy, and plans for the nuclear RMA. RMA is an imperial concept, a meta theory if you prefer.

The now long-running debate over RMA has proceeded predictably through several stages. It moved from intellectual discovery (with thanks to Soviet theorists), to conceptual elaboration and counterattack by skeptics, through some empirical investigation, to second and third thoughts, which is the condition today. Some positions have hardened, perhaps matured, over the years, as often happens in debate. For example, in a recent book, Jeremy Black, who has probably written as much about the subject of military revolutions as anyone, sought to bring down the curtain on the RMA concept once and for all. He has written that "[m]ilitary realities, however, are both too complex and too dependent on previous experiences to make the search for military revolutions helpful."[17] As usual, his argument is cogent and plausible, though I do not endorse the full measure of his skepticism. In the historians' debate about RMA, the rival poles have been represented not only by people who are friendly or unfriendly to meta narrative, but also by those who attribute greater or lesser significance to technological change. If we recall the definition of RMA offered by Andrew Krepinevich, he specified "innovative operational concepts and organizational adaptation" to exploit new technologies in "a significant number of military systems."

What happened in the debate was that despite the sophisticated and originally fairly tentative, essentially speculative view of Andrew Marshall and OSD Net Assessment, once the RMA idea became general property it was captured by a profoundly technological view of the revolution that seemed to beckon the Armed Forces into a new golden age of enhanced effectiveness.[18] This technophilia was to be expected, given America's technological strengths, its military culture, and its preferred way of war, and given the particular character of the RMA that seemed to be inviting adoption and exploitation. After all, the contemporary revolutionary change in warfare quintessentially is about the uses of the computer. Unfortunately, though again predictably, the counterblasts against the technophiles who promised to disperse "the fog of war" and such like improbable, not to say impossible, achievements, were taken too far. Scholars and analysts made the telling points that many, perhaps most, historical RMAs were led by political and social, not technological change.[19] Also, they argued, again persuasively, that organization, doctrine, and force employment, mattered rather more than did technology per se. Richard O. Hundley made that point with exceptional clarity when he wrote: "Without an operational concept, the best weapon systems in the world will never revolutionize anything."[20] He cites the early history of the machine gun in support of the point, to which one could add the French and Soviet experience with the tank in 1940 and 1941, respectively.

As was bound to happen, the assault upon the paradigm of technology-led RMA was overdone. Skepticism about the relative importance of technological innovation slipped inadvertently into what began to approach a technophobic perspective. It is time for the balance to be restored. Those of us who have written skeptically about the significance of technology for military and strategic excellence, and I count myself guilty on this count,[21] have slayed the technological dragon of such technophiles as Admiral Bill Owens, but we have proceeded intellectually way beyond "the culminating point of victory."[22]

We have drawn attention to the high importance of culture — public, strategic, and military — and have scored historically well-attested points on the vital significance of organization and operational concepts, but we need to reconsider the role and relative potency of technological change. The technophiles have lost the debate, though whether they lose in the shaping of the process of U.S. military transformation is, of course, another matter entirely. There is general agreement that how weapons are used is more important than is the quality of the weapons themselves. Similarly, it is not especially controversial to maintain that morale is the most vital factor contributing to military effectiveness. But, and it is a large but, the quality of weapons does matter. Moreover, morale, no matter how high initially, cannot be relied on to survive close lethal encounters with a better armed enemy. So many and complex are the dimensions of warfare that there will be ways to compensate for a technical shortfall. However, such compensation can be insufficient, and for preference its desperate necessity should be avoided.[23] Technology matters, even though it does not matter most.

This largely conceptual section of the monograph concludes with the posing and brisk direct answering of what seem to this theorist to be the half dozen most salient questions one can ask of the RMA concept, the notion of revolutionary change in warfare.

1. *Does the RMA concept make sense?* On balance, it does, though it should not be taken too seriously, and it can only be accepted with some reservations. Constant repetition of the RMA acronym does have a way of deadening critical faculties. It is sensible to recognize both that the character and conduct of war are always changing, and that the rate of change periodically, if irregularly, accelerates and is made manifest in somewhat nonlinear outcomes in a new way in warfare.

While it is no more than common sense to appreciate the historical reality of occasional bursts of revolutionary change in warfare, it is a little perilous to transcend such a mundane understanding and postulate RMAs. We are in danger of captivation by our own grandiose concept. After all, as a meta-narrative the RMA thesis holds that strategic history effectively has been organized and moved on by periodic revolutionary discontinuities in military affairs. There is some merit in that view, but only some. It is rather too monocausal for comfort. We should not forget that there is a subtle but important difference between the concept of RMA, and the rather less definite notion of revolutionary or radical change in warfare. As we have noted already, there is no acid test for how revolutionary or radical change needs to be before it earns the RMA badge. Recall the Krepinevich definition which holds that an RMA "alters the character and conduct of conflict . . . by producing a dramatic increase—often an order of magnitude or greater—in the combat potential and military effectiveness of armed forces." What appears to have occurred is that a large fraction of the defense community has succumbed to the reification fallacy. It has forgotten, if it ever realized, that RMA is an intellectual invention by theorists, including some historians, a profession usually quite hostile to far reaching ideas. As a consequence, there is an expectation that dramatic benefit will surely accrue, if only the United States can implement this magical procedure of an information-led RMA. Without the reified idea of an RMA, it is probable that more modest and measured expectations would attend the pursuit of a revolutionary change in warfare.

2. *Is the RMA concept useful?* The obvious answer is that surely it must be, since it has dominated American defense discourse for more than a decade. Even September 11, 2001 (9/11), and the consequent paying of extra attention to countering terrorism and to homeland security, generally failed to deflect the march towards execution of an information-led revolution in the conduct of war. However, popularity and merit are not always the same. It may be worthwhile to consider the opportunity costs of the RMA thesis. While American defense

10

professionals were earnestly and prolifically exploring and debating RMA, even in its less grandiose form simply as radical change, what were they not investigating? For one suggestion, they were not debating very usefully the strategic purposes of the mooted revolutionary change in warfare. Historically, revolutionary military changes have been task-driven. What were, and are, the tasks that foreign policy could lay upon the country's armed forces? It is difficult to resist the conclusion that in the minds of many the quest for revolutionary change, RMA, now transformation, comes perilously close to being an end in itself. As this author has argued in a recent publication, the United States has a persistent strategy deficit, rather than any dangerous incapacity to exploit the revolutionary military possibilities of information technology.[24]

3. *Does the RMA thesis much matter?* Despite the skeptical, even negative, comments just registered, the answer to this question has to be "yes." The RMA thesis holds that revolutions in warfare happen, and that they render obsolete an existing way in combat. It would be hard to exaggerate the importance of that proposition. Whether or not it is true, or true enough to warrant respect as a general verity, is another matter. A problem with the RMA thesis is that it encourages its devotees to overreach with their expectations of consequent advantage. There are two principal reasons why this should be so. First, even a genuinely revolutionary change in the conduct of warfare simply may not deliver the "dramatic increase" in military effectiveness that the Krepinevich definition promises. Moreover, even if it does so deliver, the military and strategic output may fall far short of ensuring success. There is, after all, more to war than warfare. Second, if we recall the first of the Clausewitzian epigraphs to this monograph, it is a persistent fact that warfare manifests itself in many varieties, often even within the same war. One size of revolutionary military change is unlikely to fit all cases of American strategic need.

4. *Is not change in warfare evolutionary rather than revolutionary?* An important reason why it can be difficult to recognize

and understand revolutionary change in warfare is that it is a process that must mature over time. We cannot be certain that a revolution worthy of that description has been achieved until it has been demonstrated in battle, and possibly not even then. For example, the initial German gains in their great "Michael" Offensive in March 1918 were indeed secured by means of new—at least relatively so—infantry tactics, but those tactics were flattered by the incompetence of the British defense as well as by the literal fog that compounded the usual fog of war to confuse and panic the defenders.[25] Similarly, the iconic RMA success of German arms in Flanders in May 1940 may be the exemplar of the benefit to be reaped from revolutionary change. But, as in the previous example, the potency of the German offensive depended significantly on a quite extraordinary measure of operational incompetence, on the part of the French High Command, as well as on exemplary old fashioned performance by some infantry units.[26] It would seem to be the case that the effectiveness of revolutionary change in warfare lies not, at least not only, in the new style of combat itself, as the RMA thesis claims (see the Krepinevich definition), but very much in the military and strategic contexts of its application. Changes in warfare cannot be effected overnight. They have to be the product of a process of evolution. There is an obvious circularity of argument threatening here. We can only be certain that an RMA has occurred when a revolutionary style of warfare is demonstrated successfully in battle. But, new styles of warfare do not always succeed. Once the enemy has assimilated the fact that he faces an unfamiliar style, he may be able to defeat it by a mixture of emulation and calculated evasion, always provided he has the space, which is to say the time, to do so. Recall that the standard RMA definition, see Krepinevich again, preemptively resolves the issue of desirability by specifying that military revolution produces a dramatic increase in combat potential and effectiveness. It follows from this discussion that two major difficulties impede recognition of the reality of revolutionary change. First, military capability of necessity evolves and the state of its evolution cannot be assessed with high confidence without the test of battle. Second, because war is a complex phenomenon, and warfare has many dimensions, it will not always be self-evident just why victory or defeat was the outcome. In the conventional Gulf Wars of 1991 and 2003, the U.S.-led coalition victories were hugely overdetermined.

5. *Are not continuities at least as important as changes as contributors to military effectiveness?* Naturally, a focus on revolutionary change must privilege discontinuity. Indeed, by definition, the revolutionary is expecting to secure "an order of magnitude or greater" improvement in military potential and effectiveness. Without quite challenging that view directly, it is necessary to point out that the conduct of war is a complex undertaking and even a revolutionary change in method will have only a limited domain of competence. To resort to a controversial phrase, history shows that even an apparently superior new method of war cannot compensate for errors in policy and strategy. Tactical and even operational excellence are quite meaningless save with respect to their political and strategic contextual significance. Moreover, the revolutionized military force needs to be available in decisive quantity, as well as quality, if it is to fulfil its tasks. In addition, history seems to suggest that even armies unable or unwilling to follow the RMA leader all the way to and through military revolution, sometimes are able to blunt the cutting edge of the revolutionary leader. Morale, discipline, leadership, attention to the much maligned "principles of war," an imaginative search for the distinctive vulnerabilities in a new way of war. and an imaginative effort to find offsetting advantages, are all candidate contributors to counterrevolutionary effectiveness. The potency of a revolutionary change in warfare must depend critically upon the contexts within which it is applied. Because warfare has many variants, it is improbable that a single, albeit revolutionary, change in style will be effective in all cases of potential need. The generic continuities in military activities from period to period are many and strong. Indeed, it is probably sound to believe that often there is less to gain

from some new way of fighting than there is from the reliable recovery of past skills. Counterinsurgency springs to mind as a skill set that has an uneven record as a much needed core competency of the Army.[27]

6. *Is revolutionary change in warfare the high road to victory?* The answer plainly is "no." Superior conduct of what, viewed politically and strategically, is most sensibly judged to be the wrong war, will, indeed must, produce well-merited defeat. The two finest armies of the 20th century, those of Germany in the two world wars, both lost, and lost catastrophically in the second instance. It is easy to be misunderstood. This analysis is not skeptical about, let alone hostile to, revolutionary change in warfare. What is at issue is not revolution per se, but what is asked and expected of it. The target here is neither revolutionary change, nor transformation, but rather the assumption that investment in such a venture must all but guarantee future military and strategic success. Posed thus this may be an exaggeration, but as such it helps make a vital point. We have to beware of talismanic faith in a favored vision of military revolution. Why? First, because war is multidimensional and the dimensions that we succeed in revolutionizing are likely to be outnumbered and substantially offset in their effects by behavior in the dimensions that we either have not, or cannot, change.[28] Second, it is a persisting weakness of prophets for new ways in war not to pay the enemy due respect. Thus far in this analysis, little has been said on the all important subject that war is a duel. Enemies, current and potential, could not fail to notice the emergence of a revolutionary change in the U.S. way in warfare, especially since we have spent more than 10 years debating its character and promise, and have offered mini-demonstrations in war itself. The principal danger in the years immediately ahead is that U.S. Armed Forces will be so committed to their own network-centric transformation, that they fail to recognize the true character of potentially effective offsetting revolutionary change elsewhere. As a simple matter of historical record, RMA leadership has not always led to ultimate victory in war. Hundley tells us that "*RMAs frequently bestow an enormous and*

immediate military advantage on the first nation to exploit them in combat." That is true enough, but victory is secured by the nation that wins the final combat in a conflict, not the opening round.

The Contexts of Warfare.

Warfare is all about context. It is not self-referential, autonomous behavior. Instead, it is about relative power, which is to say it is about politics. The political context is the source of, and provides the meaning for, war and its conduct in warfare. The analysis in this section does not discount the importance of military science, or of what Clausewitz called the "grammar" of war.[29] The intention here rather is to help correct an imbalance in analysis. The mission of this monograph, to contribute to the recognition and understanding of revolutionary change in warfare, addresses a subject that typically is discussed quite literally and therefore narrowly. Of course, it is important to recognize and understand changing ways in warfare in their military dimension. But, it is scarcely less important to gain the insight into the prospect of occurrence of those changing ways, as well as into the likely character of the changes, that can come only from the study of warfare's contexts.

When defense professionals strive to recognize and understand revolutionary change they need to try to leap the ethnocentric barrier and consider the strategic context from an adversary's point of view; pay full respect to the authority of the political context; recognize that revolutionary change does not necessarily deliver a step-level jump in effectiveness, just because it is new; and, finally, appreciate that warfare, as Clausewitz reminds us, can assume many forms.[30]

Happy is the defense planner who must devise ways to contend with a single kind of foe, in combat of known and predictable character, conducted by familiar methods with a stable arsenal, over issues, and in geography, that are thoroughly familiar.[31] Poor leadership, bad luck, normal friction, and so forth, may deny one victory, but at least there should be little danger of preparing for the wrong war. Alas, the U.S. situation today is maximally uncertain, in the sharpest of contrasts to the hypothetical condition just outlined.

The American superpower is committed quite explicitly to global strategic preeminence.[32] This is a logical, indeed a necessary, commitment, given the country's role as the principal armed agent of world order, the global "sheriff," as I have argued elsewhere.[33] The trouble is that the role of global guardian of order attracts hostile attention from those who would deny the United States influence in their neighborhoods.[34] The role carries obligations to intervene selectively, at least to accept some responsibilities, for maintaining or restoring order in deadly quarrels among distinctly alien societies and polities. It follows that the U.S. defense community faces two tasks of extraordinary difficulty. First, because the United States may have to dissuade, deter, and, if need be, defeat a wide range of both regular and irregular enemies, the scope of needed effectiveness placed upon the country's on-going RMA, or transformation, is exceptionally wide by any historical standard. Second, it will be challenging in the extreme for the Armed Forces to anticipate and recognize emergent alien ways in warfare that are, to a degree, purposefully asymmetrical to the new U.S. model of excellence.

It is all very well to change defense planning so that the principal driver is capability rather than threat, but for several reasons such an address-free generic approach is apt to leave the planner short-changed. Preeminently, capabilities are not always self-explanatory in an age of "unrestricted warfare."[35] Also, it is essential for defense planners to recognize that the effort to recognize and understand revolutionary change in warfare is best approached in its respective contexts. These explain why war occurs and how it is waged. It may be a revelation to many in the technology focussed U.S. defense community to realize that, historically as a general rule, military method and capability have by no means been revolutionized by technological innovations alone, or even at all in some cases.[36]

The purpose of this section of the analysis is to explore the roles of the six principal contexts of warfare, the ones that drive and shape the activity. If we are to improve our ability to recognize and understand revolutionary change, there is an acute need to look beyond military science, beyond Clausewitz's grammar of war, to the impact of change in and affecting these contexts. The contexts discussed are the political, the strategic, the social-cultural, the economic, the technological, and the geographical. Although these six are separately identifiable, naturally they influence each other. Exactly how the contexts of warfare function to trigger or enable revolutionary change will differ from episode to episode. What we discuss here is the source, or sources, of revolutionary change. In other words, if one is seeking to understand the provenance of such change, the answer lies within this framework.

1. *The political context.* This is the breeding ground of war, and hence warfare; all war and warfare we can add. If there is no political context, there can be no war. Organized violence may be criminal, or recreational-sporting, but if it is not about the relative power of political entities, not only states, it is not warfare. RMA theory can seduce the unwary into finding favor in a grand historical master narrative that at least implies near autarky for military developments. One can compose a military history of the past 2 centuries that tells the military story almost wholly in military terms. In this monograph, we suggest that such a partial perspective, though in its limited way essential, is certain to promote misunderstanding. It neglects the most important engines of change. The state of the art in military prowess is not divorced from political and social influence. Revolutionary change in methods of war do not comprise a first-order problem. Wars do not occur because of military change, revolutionary or other. The German way of war in the victory years of 1939-41 was, of course, significant, but it was of secondary importance. In the 1930s, it would have been useful for French, British, and American observers to have secured a better grasp than they did of the military meaning of Germany's innovative Panzer divisions and obsession with dive bombing.[37] But, even more profit would have flowed from an intelligent understanding of the changing political context. The problem was not the Panzer division, or even the so-called Blitzkrieg strategy, rather it was Adolf Hitler. The Third Reich was determined upon war, virtually regardless of the military method it would be obliged to pursue.[38]

As the international political context alters, so do the incentives to pursue military innovation. The end of the Cold War is of far greater significance for national and international security than is the information-led RMA. The demise of the former Union of Soviet Socialist Republics (USSR) upset the global geopolitical game board. The United States debated and, at a modest pace, proceeded to exploit the information revolution, even though it was, and remains, more than a little uncertain just what tasks will dominate the future of the military establishment. However, to recognize and understand the revolutionary military change that should be of most concern to Americans, there is an acute need to comprehend movement in the threat environment. It is not sufficient, indeed it would be foolish, to seek to recognize and understand revolutionary military change if one did not first recognize and understand the character and location of those who one may have to deter or fight. That analysis, notwithstanding its unavoidable uncertainties, will provide vital indicators to the prudent answers to the "how," "where," and "when," and "over what" questions. Achieving a good enough grasp of the dynamic political context and, one must admit, a certain luck in contingent prediction, has to be the first stage in approaching the challenge of recognizing and understanding revolutionary military change.

2. *The strategic context.* As the ever-changing political context fuels demands for military preparation and occasional action, so the strategic expresses the relationship between political demand and military supply, keyed to the particular tasks specific to a conflict. Only infrequently is the concept of strategic context defined. It tends to be simply a familiar and rather grandiose term that is rhetorically useful mainly for its very vagueness. We shall try to do better here. Bearing in mind that strategy is the bridge between political purpose, or policy, and the military instrument, we define strategic context as the tasks or missions assigned to armed forces by policy, in the light of expected difficulties and opportunities, especially those created by enemies.

Geopolitics has a lot to say about strategic context. For example, beneath, and derivative from, the political context of superpower antagonism in the Cold War was a strategic context dominated by a central geopolitical reality. Although the Soviet-American rivalry was in a sense global, ideological and ultimately territorially nonspecific, it so happened that the respective spheres of interest met around, and generally on-shore, the Rimlands of Eurasia.[39] For 40 years, the principal challenge for U.S. strategy was the need to extend a credible, or not-incredible, nuclear deterrence over allies and friends an ocean away from North America and more or less on the doorstep of the bloated Soviet imperium. This very distinctive strategic context literally drove the United States constantly to revise, at least to talk about revising, its nuclear strategy in the hope that its credibility of contingent employment might be enhanced.

It may be most sensible to conflate the political and strategic contexts, in recognition of the merit in the great man's judgment that "[t]he conduct of war, in its great outlines, is therefore policy itself."[40] Nonetheless, in this analysis, we prefer to keep strategy in clear focus, while appreciating its vital bridging function.[41] It is not too much of a challenge to explain the significance of strategic context for the mission of this monograph. If we ask the direct questions, "Where might revolutionary change in warfare come from? Where should we look?" — the leading answers must lie, first, in the political context as the sine qua non, and, second, in the strategic context that derives from the political. What are the strategic relations, the problems and opportunities, implicit in a particular political context?

3. *The social-cultural context.* Warfare has many dimensions, and the most potent are included in this admittedly somewhat brutally conflated super category. We must emphasize the fact of complex interpretation. Although we isolate six contexts here for convenience, history does not work along neatly separate grooves. They are all variably significant, and influencing each other, simultaneously. As this author has argued for many years, strategic study has to be conducted holistically. On a cognate matter, "[t]he strategic elements that affect the use of engagements," Clausewitz identified just five types: "the moral, the physical, the mathematical, the geographical, and the statistical."[42] But, he issued a stern and grim warning.

> It would however be disastrous to try to develop an understanding of strategy by analyzing these factors in isolation, since they are usually interconnected in each military action in manifold and intricate ways. A dreary analytical labyrinth would result . . .[43]

Social-cultural trends are likely to prove more revealing at an early stage of the prospects for revolutionary change in warfare than will missile tests, defense contracts, military maneuvers, or even, possibly, some limited demonstration of a novel prowess in combat. Consider the information-led RMA that is the heart and soul at least of some people's vision of transformation. It is true that the U.S. Army understands that transformation is about soldiers, people, as armies always have been.[44] But that ancient truth is not accepted universally, except nominally.

The current policy on transformation, which, at DOD level at least, is very much a high technology story, is a direct reflection of the trends in American society.[45] There is some obvious merit in the Tofflers' rather basic claim that societies fight in approximately the same manner that they produce wealth.[46] When America was preponderantly an industrial society, it waged industrial-age war on a scale in World War II that confounded foes and astonished allies. Now that America is evolving into a post-industrial society, wherein the manipulation of information is the key to prosperity, so, naturally enough, the Armed Forces must reflect that emerging reality.

Consider another example of the social-cultural roots of revolutionary change in warfare. The comparatively recent contemporary phenomenon of religiously motivated irregular warfare, including terrorism, was plainly detectable in the course and outcome of the war waged in Afghanistan against the foreign Soviet atheists in the 1980s. With the uplifting example of the Iranian Revolution of 1979, followed by the demonstrated potency of holy warriors in defeating a superpower, albeit with some vital arms provided by other unbelievers, it should not have come as a great surprise to find that military revolution might follow.[47] In the 1990s, most American defense professionals were debating eagerly what is, and what is not, an RMA. But in the Middle East, a revolutionary change in warfare was brewing as an Islamic revival of an extreme fundamentalist kind met up with, and exploited, the tools of the information age.

It is important to recognize that the social-cultural engine for revolutionary change in warfare works in two ways. On the one hand, it can, and typically will, shape the character of the revolution attainable. On the other, society and its dominant beliefs will provide the fuel for the political decisions, the policy, that actually produce the military revolution as well as the exercise of that revolution in war. It may be worth considering the possible implications of the point that revolutionary change in methods of war are, by definition, extraordinary events. They are undertaken only for the most serious of reasons. RMAs are certain to be hugely disruptive, they are probably very expensive, and, being revolutionary, they are bound to be fraught with uncertainty over effectiveness. This discussion leads inexorably to the argument that, as with arms race analysis, the political and the social-cultural always have pride of place in causation over the grammar of war. In the 1930s, the democracies would have been well-advised to study the bizarre ideology of the curious new German führer and the steps by which he and his gang of opportunists eventually secured a total grip upon society and its common assumptions.[48] Of course, the evolution of German military method mattered, but that was only because of a public culture, as made manifest in what passed for policy, that would send it into open-ended battle.

Many people have noticed that, in its understandable fascination with the potential for revolutionary change in warfare and now its commitment to the long-term execution of such change in a process of military transformation, the defense community has paid too little attention to what amounts to a social and cultural transformation in Western public attitudes towards war and warfare. Edward Luttwak rang this bell loudly with his articles in the mid-1990s on the dawning of an age of what he descriptively called "post-heroic warfare."[49] Cultural assumptions about war, its legitimacy, its proper conduct, and its utility can play a crucial role in strategic history. We must repeat the points that societies, not only states and other polities, wage war, and that there is much more to war than warfare itself, which is to say war's grammar. When we scan the strategic landscape for evidence of revolutionary change, it is essential not to neglect the social context, domestic and foreign.[50] The attitude of our society to war and warfare, and especially to casualties, could have radical implications for the range of acceptable military methods available to our generals. It is a matter of notable significance that other societies, with different cultures, will not share all, or in some cases even many, of the cultural assumptions of America.

4. *The economic context.* Wars are rarely waged for economic reasons, popular beliefs to the contrary notwithstanding, and granting some colonial exceptions. But, warfare is economic behavior, *inter alia*, just as it is, and has to be, logistical behavior also. Revolutionary change in warfare does not require an enabling economic revolution

because the change in question may not depend critically upon a radical alteration in the use of material resources. However, societies that "take off" industrially and then are locked into a temporally indefinite process of scientific, industrial and agricultural progress, typically will develop foreign interests, responsibilities, and a sense of relative self-importance that is near certain to require military expression. There are no laws of political and strategic behavior at all comparable to the laws of the natural sciences. But we can hazard as a quasi-law, a solid item of lore perhaps, the axiom that new-found economic strength breeds political ambition, which must have a strategic context, which will have implications for military posture. This is not to deny that revolutionary change in warfare can be attempted, even effected, by the economically challenged. Such revolutionaries must seek in desperation to find ways to fight smarter, certainly more cheaply than their richer enemies. All that we claim here is that ways in warfare, revolutionary and other, have an economic context. Although not as significant as the political, strategic, or social-cultural, still the economic context can provide a valuable source of warning of possible, or even probable, future strategic problems. For the most obvious of contemporary examples, the Chinese rate of economic growth has it well on the road to true super-statehood. There are a number of reasons, some excellent, some less so, why the fragility of China's export-led prosperity should discourage it powerfully from staging a serious challenge to American military hegemony. However, the strategic history of the past 2 centuries attests conclusively to the total unreliability of economic rationality as a predictor of state behavior. All that we claim here is that political and military greatness requires the underpinning of economic greatness. A polity rising economically very rapidly cannot help but acquire the means to afford a significant jump in its military capabilities. Since it will be coming up from behind in the competitive stakes, it is certain to be motivated to try to identify ways to achieve short cuts to shared military effectiveness. In other words, China, for example, is an ideal customer for new ways in warfare. Despite its inevitable flaws in prediction, Paul Kennedy's 1987 historical blockbuster, *The Rise and Fall of the Great Powers*, tells an essentially economic story that warrants respect.[51] Political and strategic history is economic history also.

5. *The technological context.* Warfare always has a technological context, but that context is not always the principal fuel for revolutionary change. Scholars have highlighted this lesson of experience by distinguishing between a Military Technical Revolution (MTR) and an RMA.[52] The MTR is simply a technology-led RMA. This was the idea that so exercised Soviet analysts in the 1970s and early 1980s, especially in the truly prescient form of the "reconnaissance-strike complex." That particular Soviet high-technology vision of future warfare is all but indistinguishable from the cutting edge of the technological dimensions to the American military transformation of the 2000s. What did the regular warfare in Afghanistan and Iraq in 2001 and 2003 showcase, if not an excellence in Command, Control, Communications, Computing, Intelligence, Targeting and Reconnaissance (C[4]ISTAR)? To which, in recognition of Stephen Biddle's careful review of military events, one must add the perennial favorite, combined arms.[53] Although Andrew Marshall and his Office broadened the Soviet-sourced concept of MTR to RMA, recognizing the importance of organization, operational concepts, and numbers, contemporary American awareness of, and interest in, the possibility of revolutionary military change has always had a powerful technological motor. This has been inevitable and, up to a point, desirable. After all, the spark which has lit the current rash of technological fires has been the exponential growth in computing capacity. Moreover, technological seers advise that there is no plausible scientific or engineering reason why Moore's Law should be falsified in this century.[54]

Obviously there are profound differences among the Services in their relative dependence upon, and hence attitude towards, technology. Whereas sailors man ships and airmen fly aircraft, soldiers *use* equipment. The quality of technology literally can be a matter of life and death to sailors and airmen. Soldiers, operating in a more complex geography, often have more choices to help them compensate for some, though only some, technological shortfalls.

Appreciation of war's changing technological context is an essential intelligence function, as well as a vital source of inspiration for domestic change. But a common material context across societies does not equate necessarily to a common understanding of the scale, or character, of the change that may be on offer. Recent studies have supported strongly what some of us have long believed or suspected. Different public, strategic, and military cultures, given their unique strategic contexts, exploit, and pick and choose among new technologies according to their own criteria of utility, not in obedience to some presumed universal military logic. If we consider the mechanization RMA(s) of the period 1930-45, for example, it is clear beyond a shadow of a doubt that notwithstanding a tolerably common technological base, each of the principal combatants in World War II developed air and mechanized ground forces along nationally distinctive lines, for reasons that appeared to make sense for each polity's strategic and military situation.[55] There should be little need to highlight the significance of this argument for the mission of our monograph. Many, and probably most, military technologies lend themselves to varied employment, depending on the local military tasks and strategic context and the preferences in operational concepts and organization. Identifying technological trends, no matter how accurately, is no guarantee of a grasp of their meaning. One could make much the same point by observing that superb overhead reconnaissance will provide formidable detail on people and their movement. Unfortunately, that intelligence can tell one nothing at all about what is in their hearts and minds.

Paradoxically, the more firmly an RMA leader, such as the United States with information technology, becomes wedded to a distinctive and arguably revolutionary paradigm of future warfare, the more likely is it to misread the character of military change abroad. It is difficult for a proud and self-confidently dominant military power to accept the notion that there can be more than one contemporary military enlightenment.[56] The strategic sin of ethnocentricity is readily revealed. First, other military cultures may not agree with the dominant power's military logic. Second, those other cultures, even if they appreciate the sense in the RMA leader's choices, will be bound to make their own decisions on investment in innovation, based upon such local circumstances as distinctive military tasking, affordability, and the need to offset the RMA leader's putative advantages.[57]

As the Parthian shot in this discussion, it is worth noting that, despite the contrary claims and implications of dozens of television series, the technological dimension to warfare is very rarely decisive. War is complex and so is its conduct in warfare. Just as its outbreak typically is the product of redundant causation, so its course and outcome, no less typically, is hardly ever plausibly, let alone unarguably, attributable to a technological advantage. It is easy to see why this should be so. Given war's complexity and the large number of dimensions that are always in play, of which the technological is only one, there are simply too many factors other than the technological which must influence events. This is a long familiar truth. For example, a recent study of Alexander the Great and his way of war concludes that although his army was "a well-armed force . . . not too much should be made of the technological edge it enjoyed over most of its enemies."[58] The author explains as follows:

> In the close-order combat of this period [4th century BC], the tactical prowess and morale of the forces was more important to the outcome of battles. Technology does not win wars. Even on those occasions when technology was clearly very significant, for example in the use of siege engines, breaches in the enemy's defences still had to be exploited by Alexander's men in face-to-face combat with the enemy. However good Alexander's instrument was, this outstanding army still had to be led and handled effectively.[59]

The subject of David Lonsdale's book may be Alexander, but his analysis has more than minor contemporary relevance.

6. *The geographical context.* No study of warfare can afford to neglect the geographical context. Time after time over the past century, military revolution keyed to the emerging exploitation of a new geographical environment has beckoned both the visionary theorist and the bold military professional. Since 1900, RMA anticipators and spotters, had there been such in those times, would have been obliged to recognize and try to understand the meaning of *submarines*, for a potential revolution in sea warfare; *aircraft*, for a potential revolution (a) in warfare as a whole, (b) in warfare on land, and (c) in warfare to, at, and from the sea; *spacecraft*, for a potential revolution, with aircraft, in warfare as a whole as well as in each of the terrestrial geographies; and, finally, the computer as *cyberpower*. History lends itself to inconveniently alternative explanations. But there can be no argument that there has been no historical precedent for the scale

25

and diversity of the challenges posed by the geographical expansion of warfare since 1900. Over the past 100 years, defense analysts, strategic theorists, and the soldiers and sailors who would be at most immediate risk at the sharp end of it all, have had to contend with the promise and peril of no fewer than four new environments (including the undersea). So familiar are we with the concept of airpower, even spacepower, and now—just about—cyberpower, that we are apt to forget how novel are, and have been, the modern geographical challenges to the comprehension of military and strategic affairs. From a time before recorded history, humans had waged war in only two dimensions, on land and on the surface of the sea. For us to have added no fewer than four geographical environments to those traditional two in less than a century, one may register as progress, or, less optimistically, at least as monumental cumulative change. But how revolutionary would the submarine, the aircraft, the earth satellite, and the computer prove to be? It is sobering to realize that even today, 102 years from the first flight of a heavier-than-air vehicle, and 94 years since Italian Lieutenant Gavotti engaged in the first act of aerial bombing in war on November 1, 1911, against the Turks in Libya, the quality of the airpower RMA remains controversial.

Thus far, this discussion has stressed the challenge in the novelty of the expansion of warfare's geography. It is necessary, however, to balance that analysis with recognition of some of the more permanent features of the geographical context. Such recognition is vital for our mission because the subject of this enquiry privileges radical change and always threatens to drive into the shadows the more significant contextual elements that change either not at all or only slowly. While certainly it is necessary to attempt to recognize and try to understand revolutionary change in warfare, it is scarcely less important to recognize and understand the constants, or very-slow-to-change variables. The latter concern can be controversial. There is a history of the advocates of military revolution claiming that their favored new method of war, exploiting a new geography, would certainly render obsolescent, then obsolete, older concerns tied to the other geographies. This has been the pattern of claims from the submarine, to the aircraft, to the satellite, and now to the computer. Cyberspace, we have been told, not only shrinks space and therefore time, it is effectively beyond geography, it exists everywhere and in a sense, therefore, nowhere.[60] If strategic information warfare is the revolution that is coming, who cares about terrestrial geographies! If "command of the nets" is the decisive enabler of victory in future warfare, as Bruce Berkowitz maintains, physical geography cannot fail to suffer a marked demotion in strategic significance.[61]

Through the several RMAs of the past century, up to and including the current exploitation of the computer, the geographical context has retained features whose importance has scarcely been scratched by revolution. Notwithstanding the marvels of submarines, aircraft, spacecraft, and computers, humans are land animals and, functionally viewed, war is about the control of their will. In the timeless and priceless words of Rear Admiral J. C. Wylie, USN: "*The ultimate determinant in war is the man on the scene with the gun.*[62] This man is the final power in war. He is control." Military revolutionaries, whether they dream of decisive mechanized maneuver, bombardment from altitude, or electronically triggered mass disruption, should never be permitted to forget Wylie's maxim. It is perhaps strange to record that in our enthusiasm for novelty, especially for that of a technical kind, we can forget both what war is about as well as who wages it. War is about politics and warfare always is about people, and people inhabit and relate to a geographical context.

Another more controversial aspect to the salience of physical geography is what we call the geopolitical. It so happens that the arrangements of continents, oceans, and islands is what it is. It is undeniable that changes in warfare, and especially in the technologies of communication, have altered the meaning of geographical distance, and hence time. But there is much, indeed there is very much, of a geopolitical character in warfare's geographical context that alters hardly at all.[63] National geographical location continues to matter greatly. That location literally dictates the necessary balance among a polity's military instruments, it determines the identity of neighbors, it translates into a distinctive history and culture, and it provides strategic opportunity and carries implicit strategic perils. Despite the wonders of network-centric warfare (NCW) and effects based operations (EBO), there are, and will long remain, significant differences between combat in the jungle, the desert, the mountains, and the city. This is not to suggest that an information-leveraging military transformation will not be able to improve performance in all environments. It is to suggest, though, that a prudent process of transformation must be flexible, adaptable, and ever mindful of the eternal fact that war is not about the enemy's military defeat, necessary though that usually will be. Instead, war is about persuading the enemy that he is defeated; to repeat, it is about influencing his will. Warfare is all about human behavior, ours and theirs. Every RMA, actual or mooted, is no more than a means to affect the minds of the people in our gunsights. Those people live in physical geography, and whether we traverse that geography hypersonically or at marching pace is really only a detail. As I have argued elsewhere, all politics is geopolitics and all strategy has to be geostrategy.[64] Not everyone is convinced, but I am hopeful that a better appreciation of the enduring significance of geography is achievable.

Revolutionary Change in Warfare: Findings and Implications.

As promised at the outset, this monograph concludes with what amounts to an audit, a critical review, of our understanding of the RMA concept and phenomenon. This should have important implications for national security policy in general, as well as for the U.S. Army in particular. The information-led revolution in question here has been advancing, initially slowly, for more than 30 years. We can argue over whether the Gulf War of 1991 was the last war of the industrial age or the first one of the information era. But it is a matter of public record that that conflict alerted the world to the fact that regular conventional warfare was changing in potentially radical ways.[65] The RMA concept emerged from the brew consisting of monitored Soviet analyses, mentioned already; a decade-plus of research and development effort to find technological offsets to Soviet mechanized strength, tactics, and inferred operational designs in Europe, hence the quest for long-range precision strike and stealthy delivery; the dramatic evidence of a new way in war that was much advertised in briefings on the victory in 1991; and the historians' debate, with their somewhat arcane, not to say parochial, controversies over what were, and what were not, historical RMAs. Today, both policy towards, and intellectual understanding of, revolutionary change in warfare are sufficiently mature for it to be feasible to attempt a critical summary of the "findings" of the years of controversy. More to the point, it is possible to suggest the implications of those findings for U.S. policy, strategy, and, generally, for the American "way of war" in the future.

It is my strong belief that each of the seven findings of this enquiry is plausible historically. By and large, this analysis has avoided argument about the use of history. However, some recent statements of a skeptical kind require an answer, primarily because I wish to insist that this monograph rests upon empirical research by some excellent historians. It is not simply an exercise in deductive strategic theory, let alone in commonsense reasoning untroubled by issues of evidence. Historian John Vincent, with typical directness, claims that "History is about evidence. It is also about other things: hunches, imagination, interpretation, guesswork. First and foremost, though, comes evidence: no evidence, no history."[66]

Vincent proceeds to explain just how partial is the evidence available. In particular, he draws attention to the facts that the winners tend to write the histories and that the "facts" are, of course, selected to tell the stories that the historians intend. And then there is the problem that most of the potential documentary evidence has not survived the rigors of deliberate omission, purposeful destruction, war, fire, flood, age, and other maladies. This author is distressed to notice that a judicious skepticism about the use of history is slipping into outright disdain. No less authoritative a publication than the *Strategic Survey 2004/05* of the International Institute for Strategic Studies (IISS) offered some thoughts frankly dismissive of historical study and history-based theory.

> The foundation of sound defence planning is identifying the operational problems of greatest potential consequence. As the preceding discussion suggests, this cannot be done by studying past RMAs or ruminating on the nature of transformation. It can be done by assessing the international environment and how trends therein might impinge on national objectives.[67]

That critic is right to excoriate scholastic theorizing, but the suggestion that our past experience with revolutionary change in warfare is irrelevant to the challenges of today could not be more wrong.[68] The major difficulty with the history constructed by historians as they seek to explain the past, has been well-expressed by Antulio J. Echevarria.

> The fundamental problem for historians is that, aside from being able to refer to such demonstrable facts as do exist, they have no *objective* references for determining (beyond a reasonable doubt) to what extent the histories they write either capture or deviate from the past. Put differently, they have nothing resembling the scientific method to aid them in determining whether what they have written is somewhat right, mostly right, or altogether wrong about the past.[69]

Which is true enough. It is also just the way that history has to be. Unfortunately, what the IISS's author would dismiss and Dr. Echevarria identifies as inescapably subjective, happens to be the whole, the sum, of human experience. Echevarria's point is not really an argument, it is simply a description of reality. Historical debate cannot be settled by reproducible experiments, period! His caveat is especially relevant to the subject of this monograph because our topic is not only change in warfare, but the challenge in recognizing and understanding such change. And how do we test for a revolution? By the degree of its change from past practice? — what degree is that? — or by its outcome? But, there is no necessary connection between RMA and victory.

Undaunted by the admitted problems with historical evidence, this monograph urges readers to accept the world of learning as it is, deficiencies and all. There is no good alternative to our seeking education from the past. Of course, we cannot find detailed guidance from past practice, but the structural continuities in human strategic experience are massive and pervasive. There have been a succession of revolutionary, indeed transformative, changes in warfare since the early 19th century. Is it plausible to argue that we have nothing to learn from that experience? The question all but answers itself. In short, although fully aware of the inherent subjectivity of historians' endeavors, this author makes no apology for offering "findings" which, if not quite demonstrably true, certainly are both well enough attested and highly plausible.

As the Army moves forward with its *Transformation Roadmap* and its subsequent editions and variants, it should derive advantage from taking heed of the seven "findings" presented below.[70] These have been chosen for their high plausibility, for their significance, and because they each have practical implications for desirable American attitudes and behavior.

1. *Contexts rule!* The central message of this monograph is that war's contexts tell most of the story. The political context is what war, warfare, and revolutionary change in either or both is all about. The strategic context derives strictly from the political, while the social-cultural, economic, technological and geographical all have more or less to say about the bounds of feasibility. After all, strategy for the conduct of war is "the art of the possible," *inter alia*.[71] The discussion of just six contexts of war and warfare is a deliberately drastic exercise in parsimony. I have accorded context the prominence it enjoys in this enquiry for two principal reasons. First, simply for its dominant role: its overriding significance mandates a position on the right of the line that it is granted here. Second, it is necessary to highlight the authority of the contexts of war, especially the political, to the American defense community, because typically the U.S. Armed Forces are much stronger in advancing warfare's "grammar" than they are in appreciating war in the round. The relevant motto quoted already is that there is more to war than warfare. As the Army moves down the path of revolutionary change for transformative effect, hopefully adaptively, the nonmilitary contexts that give meaning to and indeed, enable, the whole endeavor, assume ever greater significance. The full complexity of the contexts and dimensions of warfare are felt by armies to a far greater extent than by navies or air forces, which must operate in uninhabited, indeed uninhabitable, geographies.

The future of the U.S. Army will be driven not so much by the transformative drive, but rather by the political and strategic contexts that will shape its missions and tasks. That future is not in the hands of some reified Science of War, no matter how expertly determined by our more scientifically inclined theorists and analysts. Rather is the Army's future at the mercy of the answers to such questions as "will China assemble an anti-American coalition to contest global leadership?" — and "will America's enemies principally be irregular in character for decades to come, with the implication that the

31

Army should transform itself in such a way as to privilege COIN [counterinsurgency] as the most core of its competencies?"

The implication of this first and admittedly less than startling finding is that the Army needs to improve its understanding of war and its contexts, at the same time that it pursues its military-technical modernization.

2. *Revolutionary change in warfare may be less important than is revolutionary change in attitudes to war and the military.* While the U.S. military establishment has been planning and beginning to implement a revolutionary change in its capabilities for warfare, it probably has been behind the curve in understanding revolutionary change in the social-cultural context of the institution of war. Too much can be made of this argument, as some theorists have demonstrated. However, it is plausible to argue that two revolutions are underway; one in warfare, the subject of the protracted debate over RMA and then transformation; and one in the social-cultural context of war.[72] Although war has a constant nature through all periods, attitudes to its legitimacy and to its right conduct have been highly variable. U.S. fighter-bombers happily massacred the German forces who were striving desperately to escape from Normandy through the "Falaise Gap" in August 1944. By contrast, the United States wielded an air arm in 1991 that it felt obliged to rein-in, not that the airmen themselves were enthusiastic, from the historical replay of "Falaise" that was unfolding on the so-called "highway of death" leading north from Kuwait City. Standards of acceptable military behavior vary over time, from conflict to conflict, and sometimes within the same war against different enemies. The reasons are in part political-pragmatic, as the conduct of war is scrutinized by the media with an immediacy and in a detail that is historically unprecedented.[73] This process began as long ago as the 1850s in the Crimea. It was the result of greater public literacy, and hence the demand for more news, the creation of the new profession of war correspondent, the invention of the electric telegraph, and, of course, the slow growth of democratic politics which engendered a sense of public involvement in the country's strategic ventures and adventures.[74]

Some theorists today believe that the RMA which is the responsibility of the U.S. defense establishment to effect is really of less significance than is a Revolution in Attitudes towards the Military, or RAM. The future American way(s) of war, singular or plural, will be shaped by the social and cultural context which defines the bounds of acceptable military behavior, as well as by the military-technical opportunities that beckon as a consequence of the exploitation of information technology.

By way of an extreme, but telling example of the potency of this second finding, consider the character of the Soviet-German War (within a war) of 1941-45. While one must explain the scale of the struggle in terms of the extraordinary strength of the combatants, the breathtaking brutality of what was, truly, a total war, owed much less to the military methods of the belligerents than it did to the rival ideologies and the finality of the stakes: it was literally victory or death. It is plausible to argue that Germany might well have won its war in the East had the social and cultural context of that conflict not been defined by the Nazi leadership as a struggle for racial survival.

The plain implication of this finding is that revolutionary change in warfare is always much more than a narrowly military matter. What is more, social and cultural contexts differ among societies. It is not safe to assume that strategic behavior deemed morally unacceptable by our society would meet with identical prohibition abroad.

Although this analysis registers strong approval of the new-found official significance attached to war's social and cultural dimension, two caveats need to be noted. It is all too easy to seize on a fashionable, and basically prudent, idea and respond with a "me, too," without really considering the implications. First, it is noticeable that in the current discourse on defense policy, recognition of the relevance of "culture" has become a part of the necessary canon of right beliefs. As such, it is in danger of evolving rapidly, if it has not already done so, from an excellent idea into little more than a panacea.[75] In the latter case, it is being touted as *the answer* to America's military and strategic difficulties when intervening in alien societies. But, it is not the answer, it is only a part of the answer. The second caveat is to remind the Army that it commands warriors, not cultural anthropologists. Of course, it is important to understand the enemy, and one's friends as well, but armies are, at root, about fighting. Given the global domain of America's ordering interests, it is thoroughly impractical to expect more than a small number of military specialists to acquire a deep knowledge of the relevant local societies with their values, beliefs, languages, and histories. Since tens of thousands of distinctly nonacademic young American warriors may be transported on short notice to surprising foreign locations, the idea that "culture-centric warfare" is the, or even a, way to go, does not appear to this theorist to be a very practical suggestion. It is not so much a question of inherent desirability, simply of feasibility. Our soldiers have to be expert at fighting; cultural skills, though important, are secondary.

3. *Historical research shows that there are vital conditions for success in carrying through revolutionary changes in warfare.* At some risk of placing an undue burden of explanation on a single body of research, this analysis is impressed by a particular set of case studies of RMA and by its editors' conclusions—*The Dynamics of Military Revolution, 1300-2050,* edited by MacGregor Knox and Williamson Murray. These editors suggest that "[p]ast revolutions in military affairs have given evidence of at least four distinguishing characteristics."[76] It need hardly be said that since the mission of this monograph is to help the Army recognize and understand revolutionary change in warfare, it is deeply interested in what historians can teach. It is interesting to note that the distinguished subject experts assembled by the editors did come up with a set of explanations that made for a coherent story, overall, notwithstanding the on-going, quite bitter "historians' debate" about RMA cited earlier.[77]

On the authority of eight case studies ranging from the 14th century to 1940 (the "2050" in the book's title is seriously inappropriate), one should add as well other studies they have conducted;[78] Knox and Murray make four historically founded claims about RMAs. They argue, first, that "technology alone has rarely driven them; it has functioned above all as a catalyst." Second, they argue that,

> revolutions in military affairs have emerged from evolutionary problem-solving directed at specific operational and tactical issues in a specific theatre of war against a specific enemy. Successful innovators have always thought in terms of fighting wars against *actual* rather than *hypothetical* opponents, with *actual* capabilities, in pursuit of *actual* strategic and political objectives.

Third, the editors claim that "such revolutions require coherent frameworks of doctrine and concepts built on service cultures that are deeply *realistic*. Innovation, to be successful, must rest upon thorough understanding of the fundamentally chaotic nature of war." Fourth and finally, they assert that "revolutions in military affairs remain rooted in and limited by strategic givens and by the nature of war. *They are not a substitute for strategy*—as so often assumed by utopians—but merely an operational or tactical means."[79]

I have quoted Knox and Murray so extensively because theirs is by far the most mature, authoritatively researched, and persuasive collective statement from the historians' realm to have appeared thus far. Also, need I confess, this author agrees with their conclusions. Their edited book is especially impressive because it is authored by scholars who are, at the least, not unfriendly to the RMA thesis, while being prudently skeptical of extravagant claims for the revolutionary impact of innovative technologies. In addition, the book appeared 10 years into the long-running debate. By that time, the authors, the editors in particular, had had ample time to outgrow any early opinions that may have leaned unduly in praise or criticism of the RMA postulate when it was still relatively fresh and untried.

At this juncture, it is necessary to refer to a conceptual and contextual point that was first registered much earlier. Specifically, the conclusions to Knox and Murray just quoted need to be seen in the context of the key distinction that they themselves highlighted between RMAs and the much rarer, but vastly more traumatic, indeed unavoidable, MRs. The course and dynamic objectives of the current process of transformation are arguable. But to the extent to which this process is a broad response to the global information revolution effected by the leading information-using society, the American, it is inevitable, unstoppable, and, in a sense, beyond criticism. It simply reflects the way of the world in the 2000s.

The meaning of the Knox and Murray volume for the U.S. Armed Forces could not be clearer, at least to this convinced theorist. Despite Antulio Echevarria's potent caveat concerning the lack of objectivity in history, a judgment possibly supported by no less an authority than Sir Michael Howard, with his dismissive, and in my view misleading, truism that "history is what historians write,"[80] Knox and Murray have shown us that history can be accessible to, and useful for, policymakers and soldiers today. This is an important claim, if true. If untrue, it is still important, though in that case it is a danger. There is no law which requires one only to learn correct and appropriate things from historical experience. However, it is the view of this analysis that historical study, notwithstanding the biases and other fallibilities of historians, can make an essential, valuable contribution to the recognition and understanding of revolutionary change in warfare.

4. *Recognition of change in warfare is one thing, but understanding the character, relevance, and implications of change is something else entirely, given the sovereignty of the political and strategic contexts.* Historically, recognizing and understanding revolutionary change in warfare has been far more a matter of grasping consequences, than of existential recognition. As a general rule and for obvious reasons, would-be belligerents tend to be tolerably well-informed about the capabilities of their intended foes, though there have been many notable, and notably catastrophic, exceptions.[81]

It is unusual, to say the least, for a belligerent to be as ignorant of the enemy's military strengths as was Germany in 1941, when it invaded the USSR. German Military Intelligence, Foreign Armies East of the Army General Staff, confidently undercounted Soviet divisions initially by a wide margin and, for the future by a margin so great as almost to beggar the imagination. Naturally, there is some difficulty in comparing divisions, let alone division-equivalents. It is true that German divisions typically were more substantial than Soviet, but wartime attrition, Germany's disastrous and progressively more desperate combat manpower shortage after the 1941 Moscow campaign, as well as the lower fighting quality of Axis allied divisions, much increased the German numerical shortfalls. When Barbarossa was unleashed on June 22, 1941, Foreign Armies East estimated a total Red Army strength, in all theaters (i.e., including Asia) of approximately 240 divisions and their equivalents. They made no allowance for the quasi-army of the People's Commissariat of Internal Affairs (NKVD), which was relatively small, lightly armed, and rapidly overrun in June and July. However, the NKVD, the regime's private army, actually fielded no fewer than 53 divisions, 20 brigades, several hundred regiments of various types, as well as hundreds of smaller units with special assignments. The main fact on which Foreign Armies East was in error was that the Red Army on July 1, 1941, nominally had 281 division equivalents, not 240 or so, a figure which grew to the incredible figure of 581 by February 1, 1943, when Stalingrad fell, and which expanded to 603 by December 1 of that year. And those figures do not include NKVD forces. As to the fact cited in the text, not only was Foreign Armies East highly unreliable on the strength of the Red Army, also it had no notion of the scale of the Soviet Union's relocation of most of its armaments factories to the Urals and beyond, while it knew nothing at all about the production capacities of those factories. That is what happens when there is no aerial reconnaissance deep over the intended victim's territory (it was forbidden by high policy, and the Luffwaffe lacked planes with the necessary range), and when the Abwehr literally had no agents on the ground in that country (again, this was forbidden by policy when Hitler was wooing Stalin and, later, was not wishing to fuel his suspicions).[82] It is far more common for belligerents to be as well-informed on most of the salient facts as they are apt to be ignorant of the meaning of those facts in their particular local political and social-cultural contexts. Whether the current process of transformation is best regarded as an MR or an RMA is quite beside the vital point that no measure of military revolutionary change can alter the sovereignty of warfare's political and strategic context. Of course, military effectiveness matters. But that effectiveness has no value in and of itself. It can only be a means to political ends, via the transmission belt, the bridge, of strategy.

Logically, perhaps, it should be the case that revolutionary change in warfare can turn the political context into a dependent variable. But, do policymakers shape decisions favoring war because they believe that they have on hand a reliable military tool? Perhaps very occasionally this occurs. But, far more often than not the will to fight, and the decision, precedes confidence in the promise of a new military instrument. If historians are prone to believe the evidence that suits them, so, too, are policymakers. Some excellent recent studies by historians cast more than a little doubt on the popular long-standing image of the military professionals of the mid-to-late 19th century and the first half of the 20th as ignorant buffoons, men as baffled by new technology as they were careless of the lives of their men. The truth, to resort to that invaluable anti-post-modern concept, is that the past, present, and presumably the future, of war and warfare is hugely diverse, and most telling examples can be challenged by counterexamples. In fact, examples of professional military prescience and its obverse will both be sound. For the limited purpose of this enquiry, however, it is sufficient simply to note the rich variety of accuracy and error by historical figures.

It should be instructive for us to note that the myth of the "short war illusion" was not shared by the most senior military leaders of the principal belligerents of 1914. They were convinced that a great-power war could not fail to expand to be a general conflict, one that would engage the efforts of the whole of society, a people's war, as the Franco-Prussian War became *after* the defeat of the regular French Army. As for the style in warfare appropriate for the conditions of the 1910s, as Dr. Antulio Echevarria has shown beyond reasonable challenge, the German Army had attained a good understanding of the meaning of modern civilian and military technologies, in their social context, and had proceeded to write excellent tactical doctrine which expressed that understanding. The trouble was that, notwithstanding the legendary superiority of German training methods, many commanders in 1914 ignored the new drills, with lethal consequences for their poorly prepared *landsers*.[83]

To move forward rapidly in time, the U.S. Armed Forces today know that they do, and will long continue to, face strategically highly asymmetric, culturally alien enemies. At long last culture "has made it," as a recognized dimension known to be important to the success of transformed forces in action, or even in deterrence. But to recognize that culture matters is not quite the same as knowing how it matters or what we should do with the cultural knowledge acquired—and acquired by whom? The theater military planners and the soldiers on the ground will need cultural enlightenment, not only the policymakers in Washington. This point intersects the main thrust of the enquiry, because it means that even if we grasp well the notional military potency of our transforming forces, we could still be horribly in error. To recite the theme tune of this analysis, "contexts rule!" The effectiveness of a revolutionary American way of war will not be wholly within America's competence to ensure. Americans may wage the wrong war the wrong way, or the right war the wrong way, because they failed to recognize and understand the political and cultural context of the conflict at issue. This is not by any means intended as a counsel of despair. It is simply a warning, indeed it is a lesson from history, to deploy the old fashioned idea.

Our public, strategic, and military cultures contribute mightily to the strategic and military choices we make, and they also, inevitably, constitute an ideational prism through which we regard the behavior of other cultures.[84] To see foreign strategic behavior as its foreign authors see it, readily can overstretch our particularly encultured strategic imagination. An important recent study of the performance of U.S. intelligence in spotting foreign military innovation in the interwar years, written by Thomas C. Mahnken, offers conclusions highly relevant to this enquiry. He finds that U.S. intelligence was substantially the victim of its preconceptions.[85] A cognate idea is Jeremy Black's deployment and use of the notion of cultural assumptions.[86] Mahnken discovered, perhaps unsurprisingly, that foreign military innovation was most likely to be identified when it fitted what Americans were predisposed to expect, it had already been demonstrated in battle, or when it was development that was also of interest to the U.S. Armed Services. Overall, Mahnken's excellent study warns us that it is difficult to spot military innovations, or to assess them realistically, if they are unfamiliar, if they are familiar but not favored by us, or if they are generally despised as unpromising or worse.[87] Given the mission of this monograph, to consider the challenge of recognizing and understanding revolutionary change in warfare, it is all but self-evident that predispositions and cultural assumptions can comprise a formidable barrier to understanding. Unlike 18th and 19th century European warfare, American warfare in the 21st century will engage distinctly asymmetrical foes who fight in unfamiliar ways.

5. *When we effect a revolutionary change in the way we fight, we must do so adaptably and flexibly. If we fail the adaptability test, we are begging to be caught out by the diversity and complexity of future warfare. If we lock ourselves into a way of warfare that is highly potent only across a narrow range of operational taskings, we will wound our ability to recognize and understand other varieties of radical change in warfare. Moreover, we will be slow, if able at all in a relevant time span, to respond to them.* As we have had occasion to mention before, both in an epigraph and in the

text, Clausewitz tells us that "war is more than a true chameleon that slightly adapts its characteristics to the given case."[88] He proceeds to comment that we need a theory able to accommodate the all too rich diversity of war's variable character. Before advancing the argument with the theory of the Great Prussian, it is only fair to alert readers to a recent full-frontal challenge mounted by Britain's most popular military historian, Sir John Keegan. In his near instant book on the Iraq War of 2003, a work in which he was highly approving of American policy, he thoroughly misreads Clausewitz, but he does so in an interesting and timely manner. He is timely because now he is writing to an American defense community that has been rudely alerted to the realities of cultural diversity. Sir John offers the following dicta, which are worth quoting. To repeat, they are wrong about the master, but still there is a diamond lurking in the rough.

> The circumstances in Iraq in 2003 demonstrate that classical military theory applies only to the countries in which it was made, those of the advanced Western world. Elsewhere, and particularly in the artificial ex-colonial territories of the developing world usually governed as tyrannies, it does not.[89]

Keegan's opinion on the Prussian would have come as a surprise to Mao-Tse Tung, who was a strong admirer and user of his theory of war. Keegan believes that the Clausewitzian trinity is really a joke in a "country" like Iraq, and he attributes the lack of effective regular resistance to invasion in 2001 and 2003 to the absence of morale, a will to fight, among the people in the "trinity." What Keegan does not understand is that Clausewitz's trinity allows for near infinite combinations of relative influence among the three fundamental elements from historical case to case.[90]

Clausewitz reposes the heart of his theory of war in his primary trinity—a theory that has to maintain a balance between violence, hatred, and enmity; chance and probability; and the reason that should be behind policy. Clausewitz offers a potent simile when he likens the relations among his three tendencies (passion, chance and creativity, and reason) to "an object suspended between three magnets." In other words, although "all wars are things of the same nature," that nature is exceedingly permissive of variety and innovation. The implications for this analysis could hardly be plainer. Four, in particular, demand recognition.

First, while "contexts rule" is the most important of our more general findings, its military complement has to be the necessity for a United States with global strategic responsibilities to ensure that the radical change it intends in its way of war is sufficiently adaptable and flexible. Historically, successful executors of RMAs have effected change that could be exploited in different ways, against different enemies, and in different geographical conditions. No matter how wonderful the promise of a particular RMA, airpower for a classic example, if it is developed to deliver major advantage only in warfare across a narrow, albeit vitally important, range, it is going to fail the critical strategy test.[91] It will provide means inadequate to support policy. In my book, *Strategy for Chaos*, I made the argument, thus far uncontested even by the less friendly reviewers, that the implementing of an RMA, of revolutionary change in warfare, is strategic behavior.[92]

The necessity for the U.S. Army to plan, organize, train, equip, and write doctrine for an adaptable transformation can cite no clearer precedent than the experience of "the greatest military strategist of all time."[93] Alexander of Macedonia was never, repeat never, defeated in battle. He effected an RMA, building on the changes already implemented by his gifted, if notably rough-hewn, father, Philip II. Alexander enjoyed 12 years in supreme command, including most especially the 10-year-long series of campaigns to bring down and supplant the super-state of the era, Persia. Alexander's army waged war invariably ultimately victoriously against both regular and irregular enemies, against Greeks and a substantial fraction of the warrior races of Asia, over all manner of terrain, including some of the worst in the world, and in all weathers. He fought limited wars to coerce, just to influence, as well as wars of conquest. When feasible, he was pleased to allow diplomacy to secure for him by grand strategy what otherwise would have to be bought by the blood of his soldiers. It is true that the key to Alexander's success was not his RMA, rather was it the personal and national loyalties that sustained morale and his own irreplaceable genius. Nonetheless, this tale of distant strategic and military excellence, despite its highly individual human centerpiece, has major implications for this monograph.

Alexander inherited and improved a flexible combined-arms force that proved itself adaptable to the challenges posed by enemies of all kinds, some with styles of war utterly strange to the Greeks — in India for example — as well as some cunningly planned to offset Greek strengths. His army functioned well enough in all climes, and in combats great and small. What I am describing is an exemplar, perhaps the exemplar, of what the U.S. Armed Forces need to aim to be, if they are to transform so as to meet the demands of the country's ambitious "National Security Strategy." U.S. strategic needs over the next several decades will be at least as stressful as those which Alexander's army was obliged to overcome from 334 to 323 BC.

Finally, it is interesting to note that, as with Iraq in 2003, Alexander achieved regime change in Persia very swiftly, albeit bloodily. The political, strategic, and cultural challenges that that success delivered were not dissimilar to America's problem today. Having beaten the enemy, you own him! In an obvious sense, this was not a difficulty for Alexander because he had intended to own Persia, not merely to raid and loot it for its past wrongs against Greeks. Nonetheless, the basic question he faced was one familiar to us today. The regime was changed, the enemy tyrant, like Saddam Hussein, was a pitiful refugee, doomed to an ignominious demise, but what is the war, actually the wars, after the war like? When you collapse an empire, it is opportunity time for local warlords to assert their independence. Sound familiar?

Second, to implement a revolutionary change in warfare is not necessarily to command warfare's future character. To venture a contestable phrase, history appears to show that the combat effectiveness of revolutionary change depends critically upon the inadvertent cooperation of a poorly prepared enemy. The initial German assaults in March 1918, the Blitzkrieg victories of 1939-41, and even the follies of hapless Iraqis in 1991 and 2003, and Talibans in 2001, all illustrate this fact. More distantly, the armies of the French Revolution and Empire depended more on superiority of numbers, on the Emperor's operational, not so much tactical, skill, on their high reputation and morale, and on the prior demoralization of the enemy, than they did on a new way in warfare. Rather like the Union armies in the East in 1862-63, for a while, at least,[94] the enemies of France were half-defeated before ever a shot was fired. However, what if the enemy declines to cooperate physically, morally, operationally, or strategically in his own defeat? What if he seeks, and sometimes finds, a style or form of warfare that does not privilege the "way" of the revolutionary innovator? This is not to suggest that an RMA leader always can be thwarted by a materially disadvantaged foe who, of necessity, needs to try to fight smarter. But it is to maintain that, in many cases, warfare, especially when approached in the broad contexts of the pertinent war, can be prosecuted in a number of alternative ways. U.S. soldiers may believe, with some good reason, that an information-led way of war, one that enables networkcentricity and EBO, is all but omni-competent. The U.S. military competencies magnified by the intended revolutionary change should yield vital advantage in warfare of all kinds. I suggest that this is a truth with limitations. Intelligent enemies should be able to blunt the U.S. sword by attacking, not necessarily American soldiers, but rather the American style in warfare. For example, casualty creation will have obvious grand strategic, and hence political attraction. When we mention the importance of the contexts of war for the promise in innovative methods of warfare, we intend to suggest that cunning and capable enemies fight grand strategically, not only military-strategically. Wars are waged at every level. Our transforming army must never forget this.

The second implication derives not so much from the diversity of warfare, but rather from its complexity. If one asks, "What is war made of?" and "How does it all work?" the answer is depressingly complex.[95] I shall content myself here simply by citing as a fact the many dimensions of warfare and strategy. In order to maintain focus specifically on the subject of this enquiry, I challenge readers to ask themselves in what ways should the on-going U.S. military transformation enable the entire effort to achieve that "dramatic increase — often an order of magnitude or greater — in the combat potential and military effectiveness of armed forces," of which Krepinevich wrote back in 1994? Warfare may seem to be a straightforward enterprise. It is about the threat, or actuality, of killing people and breaking things for the purposes of high policy. But to achieve tolerable competence in those violent arts a vastly complex institution has to function well enough, though mercifully not perfectly. As noted already, Clausewitz identified five elements of war: moral, physical, mathematical, geographical, and statistical. In 1979, Michael Howard was even more economical; he preferred just four: the logistical, operational, social, and technological. While this author, seeking strength in numbers and ignoring the sound principle that more is usually less, has located no fewer than 17.[96] To spare this text needless detail, I will omit a few of my dimensions: people, society, culture, politics, ethics, information and intelligence, theory and doctrine, technology, military operations (fighting performance), command, geography, friction and chance, the adversary, and time. The point of importance is not to spot the correct number of dimensions, an absurdly misconceived task, or to argue about their precise identity. Instead, what matters is to recognize just how complex is the institution of war and its conduct as warfare, and therefore just how vulnerable its course can be to ambush from a wide variety of sources. Folly, incompetence, bad luck, or plain ineffectiveness on almost any of war's dimensions has the potential to make a mockery of that aspiration for a "dramatic increase" in military effectiveness to which Krepinevich pointed.

The third implication of the diversity and complexity of warfare, though primarily of the former, has been signalled lightly above. Specifically, even if one's revolutionized military machine functions as it should, the politicians say "go," the generals turn the key, and the engine starts, the new way of war may not deliver decisive victory if the political and social-cultural contexts are not permissive. This is not an argument against innovation, revolutionary or other. But it is a reminder that few, if any, military establishments are equally competent in the conduct of war of every kind. Similarly, RMAs, no matter how well-conceived and executed as prudent strategic behavior, always have their distinctive limitations. It is perhaps true to claim that the contemporary American revolution in warfare is more of a grand MR than a humble RMA or MTR. If that is the case, generic limitations should be less damaging. Nonetheless, this author suggests that the traditional American way of war, one which favors firepower and mechanical over human methods, is likely to exploit the information revolution militarily in a way that does not yield equivalent benefit in all forms of conflict.[97]

The fourth implication of the diversity and complexity of warfare is that there will often be opportunity for traditional military virtues to triumph over, or at the least embarrass, innovative virtuosity. We claimed above that military revolution could fail to deliver victory if it was executed in action in a nonpermissive political, social, or indeed strategic, context. Even if revolutionary change is effected and applied as force in permissive looking contexts, still it may not succeed. The reason lurks in those many dimensions cited above. Such old fashioned virtues as command efficiencies, discipline, training, morale, and leadership, for key examples, may suffice to blunt the cutting edge of a new way of war. Historically speaking, it is not the case that investment in revolutionary military change yields a ticket to guaranteed victory. An important reason why this should be so is the subject of the next, the penultimate, "finding" of this study.

6. *Revolutionary change in warfare always triggers a search for antidotes. Eventually, the antidotes triumph. They can take any or all of tactical, operational, strategic, or political forms. The solution is to carry through an RMA that is adaptable, flexible, and dynamic, as recommended in Finding No. 5.* Finding No. 6 rests on the claim that one cannot understand revolutionary change in warfare without taking full account of warfare's adversarial dimension. As the Prussian master insists on the first page of *On War*:

> War is nothing but a duel on a larger scale. Countless duels go to make up war, but a picture of it as a whole can be formed by imagining a pair of wrestlers. Each tries through physical force to compel the other to do his will; his *immediate* aim is to *throw* his opponent in order to make him incapable of further resistance. War is thus an act of force to compel our enemy to do our will.[98]

War is a struggle against an adversary with an independent will. Enemy-independent, or absent save as hapless victim, analysis cannot be an analysis of war. Because of war's adversarial nature, enemies, actual or potential, must always be motivated to seek antidotes somewhere amidst war's rich complexity to the threat posed by a rival's revolutionary enhancement in military effectiveness. The historical life-cycle of RMAs includes adversary response and then the counter-response, and so on in a process of interaction. What is important is to recognize that there can be no final move.[99] Every revolutionary change in warfare has met, if not its Waterloo, at least an effective enough answer. Even the MR of the nuclear revolution has been all but neutralized politically and strategically, though assuredly not militarily, by the potency of emulation that creates a condition of variably stable mutual deterrence. At least this was true enough during the First Nuclear Age of the Cold War. It is no longer so in the Second Nuclear Age, with its trickle of new regional nuclear weapon states.[100]

No polity, including the United States today, ever is permitted to enjoy for long, unchallenged, the benefits of a successful revolutionary way in warfare. This claim rests on the rock-solid basis of the anarchic structure of international politics, past, present, and, we can say with confidence, future. America's rivals cannot afford to concede military and strategic superiority, if that is what the revolution appears to yield. The idea that they can be dissuaded indefinitely from competing by the scale of the task America poses, is, alas, a fantasy. This author is reminded of the old saying that "the difficult we do immediately; the impossible takes a little longer." By common discovery, imitation, theft, purchase, and espionage, especially if revolutionary change is demonstrated in war, the RMA of the day will be recognized and eventually comprehended. When feasible and judged desirable, it will be copied in parts. When borrowed, it will be domesticated to fit local cultural preferences and strategic circumstances.[101] If it cannot or should not be imitated, then the challenge will be to find ways of warfare that negate much of its potential. Common sense should tell us that this must be so, but happily we need not rely solely on that unreliable source of authority. In the conclusions to their edited work on military revolutions, Murray and Knox deliver the unqualified verdict that "[e]very RMA summons up, whether soon or late, a panoply of direct countermeasures and 'asymmetrical responses'."[102] We have been warned.

7. *Revolutionary change in warfare is only revealed by the "audit of war," and not necessarily reliably even then. And if it is to be conducted competently, review of that audit must take full account of war's complex nature.* The core competency of a military force is the ability to apply sufficient violence that the polity's enemies lose the will and, if need

46

be, the ability, to resist further. In a long period of peace when they cannot test their prowess, military establishments tend to forget that war is their business and that fighting is their distinctive contribution to that institution. There is something to be said in favor of Murray and Knox's claim that "[o]nly the audit of war, a war conducted against a significantly backward opponent, will demonstrate that an RMA has occurred."[103] But the experience of trouncing hopeless adversaries is as likely to mislead as it is to enlighten. After all, we are not interested in revolutionary change as an end in itself, in the mere fact of its achievement. Rather are we always, and solely, concerned with understanding its consequences, which is the distinctive domain of strategy? Almost by definition, enemies who are significantly backward most probably can be defeated by virtually any moderately competent way of war. In that event, who needs an RMA?

At this concluding point in the study, I must indicate, belatedly perhaps, that, there may be some inadvertent confusion between a revolutionary change in methods of war and an order of magnitude increase in military effectiveness. Andrew Krepinevich links the two in the definition I have quoted several times. There is no doubt that the intent of revolutionaries is a "dramatic increase" in effectiveness. However, to change one's method of warfare is not *necessarily* to change one's military performance very much for the better. One might, indeed one should. But not all revolutions have revolutionary consequences, and particularly is this likely to be so in the contexts of war wherein there must be an active opponent and the nature of the activity is vastly complex. That complexity, to repeat, allows opportunities for offsetting tactics, operations, strategies, and policies.

The final thought in this lengthy enquiry is that the RMA concept, the notion of revolutionary change in means and methods, is perilously short of firepower for coping with the all too rich diversity and complexity of war. It is probable that revolutionary change, of any character, will yield dramatic advantages only along a fairly narrow stretch of the warfare spectrum. My Alexandrian example showed what has been achieved when true genius is in charge. Furthermore, it is a certainty that such change must trigger a quest for offsetting means, methods, and policies, on the part of enemies. These negative observations do not amount to a condemnation of the very concept of revolutionary change, appearances to the contrary possibly notwithstanding. Instead, they suggest that a U.S. military establishment committed to a particular vision of its modernization, would be well-advised to assess its process of change in the light cast by appreciation of the contexts of war and warfare discussed in this enquiry.

Summary of Findings.

1. Contexts rule!

2. Revolutionary change in warfare may be less important than revolutionary change in social attitudes to war and the military.

3. Historical research shows that there are vital conditions for success in carrying through revolutionary changes in warfare.

4. Recognition of change in warfare is one thing, but understanding the character, relevance, and implications of change is something else entirely, given the sovereignty of the political and strategic contexts.

5. When we effect a revolutionary change in the way we fight, we must do so adaptably and flexibly. If we fail the adaptability test, we are begging to be caught out by the diversity and complexity of future warfare. If we lock ourselves into a way of war that is highly potent only across a narrow range of strategic and military contexts, and hence operational taskings, we will wound our ability to recognize and understand other varieties of radical change in warfare. Moreover, we will be slow, if able at all in a relevant time span, to respond effectively to them.

6. Revolutionary change in warfare always triggers a search for antidotes. Eventually the antidotes triumph. They can take any or all of tactical, operational, strategic, or political forms. The solution, in principle if not always in practice, is to carry

through an RMA that is adaptable, flexible, and dynamic, as recommended in Finding No. 5.

7. Revolutionary change in warfare is only revealed by the "audit of war," and not necessarily reliably even then. And if it is to be conducted competently, review of that audit must take full account of war's complex nature.

ENDNOTES

1. Carl von Clausewitz, *On War*, Michael Howard and Peter Paret, trans., Princeton, NJ: Princeton University Press, 1976, p. 89 (hereafter cited as Clausewitz).

2. *Ibid.*, p. 606.

3. *Ibid.*, p. 54.

4. Andrew W. Marshall, *Statement on "Revolutions in 'Military Affairs',"* before the Senate Armed Services Committee, Subcommittee on Acquisition and Technology, May 5, 1995. In a letter to the author dated August 24, 1995, Dr. Marshall wrote to say that "I think the period we are in has a lot of similarities to the 20s and 30s and that we are in the early 20s. We have only the beginnings of the ideas about the appropriate concepts of operations and organizations. The innovations will be harder this time because there appear to be few new distinctive platforms." A key early document was Andrew W. Marshall, *Some Thoughts on Military Revolutions*, Memorandum for the Record, Office of the Secretary of Defense (OSD), Office of Net Assessment, July 27, 1993. Marshall sponsored the research which led to an outstanding collection of case studies on the 1920s and 1930s. See Williamson Murray and Allan R. Millett, eds., *Military Innovation in the Interwar Period*, Cambridge: Cambridge University Press, 1996.

5. For some of my earlier assessments, see Colin S. Gray, *The American Revolution in Military Affairs: An Interim Assessment*, Occasional Paper 28, Camberley, UK: The Strategic and Combat Studies Institute, 1997; and *Strategy for Chaos: Revolutions in Military Affairs and the Evidence of History*, London: Frank Cass, 2002.

6. For the record, let it be understood that this author is not hostile to the concepts of NCW and EBO. He thinks that they are excellent ideas, and, indeed, that they always have been. The problem with them is that there is a danger that these commonsensical notions have become canonized by high official blessing, and now have the status more of articles of faith than as vital and useful principles for guidance.

7. John Vincent, *History*, London: Continuum, 2005, p. 168.

8. History is ambiguous as a concept. It can refer to what happened, whether or not we are well-informed about it. But also it can refer to what historians have written. Modern intellectual fashion has tended to dismiss history as an accessible

past. Instead, we are invited to have only low expectations of the veracity in historical writing. In a recent essay, Dr. Antulio J. Echevarria characteristically corners the "the trouble with history." He tells us that, "[t]he problem is not so much that history is a 'fable agreed upon,' as Napoleon reportedly said, but that except for those accounts that blatantly contradict or disregard the available facts, the reader cannot determine *objectively* which history is more accurate than another. Ultimately, historical truth, like beauty, remains in the eye of the beholder." "The Trouble with History," *Parameters*, Vol. XXXV, No. 2, Summer 2005, p. 81 (emphasis in the original). Echevarria is right with his post-modern view. Nonetheless, I decline to be intimidated by his formidable logic, and I persist in regarding historical study as a practicable search for truth. Perhaps I should say for a plausible approach to truth. The trouble with "The Trouble with History," is that it will be read and cited to confirm anti-historical bias in a U.S. defense community not overly inclined to respect the past.

9. Williamson Murray and MacGregor Knox, "Thinking About Revolutions in Warfare," in Knox and Murray, eds., *The Dynamics of Military Revolution, 1300-2050*, Cambridge: Cambridge University Press, 2001, pp. 12, 7.

10. Andrew F. Krepinevich, "Cavalry to Computer: The Pattern of Military Revolutions," *The National Interest*, No. 37, Fall 1994, p. 30.

11. Richard O. Hundley, *Past Revolutions, Future Transformation: What can the history of revolutions in military affairs tell us about transforming the U.S. Military?* MR-1029-DARPA, Santa Monica, CA: RAND, 1999, p. 9. Mercifully, this study is untroubled by post-modern qualifications of judgment.

12. *Ibid.*

13. *Ibid.*

14. Jeremy Black, "A Military Revolution? A 1660-1792 Perspective," in Clifford J. Rogers, ed., *The Military Revolution Debate: Readings on the Military Transformation of Early Modern Europe*, Boulder, CO: Westview Press, 1995, p. 98.

15. It is worth noting that Black's objection to the RMA concept is not of the post-modernist kind. He writes with some confidence in the belief that the past is accessible to our understanding. Moreover, in common with this theorist, Black does not subscribe to the view that "history" is a beauty contest between competing fables.

16. The United States declares that it is a country at war, a commitment that flatters the contemporary foe more than a little. No matter how impressed one may be by the prowess of whatever al Qaeda is today, its menace does not, and will never, bear even a remote resemblance to that posed by the Soviet Union.

17. Jeremy Black, *Rethinking Military History*, London: Routledge, p. 225.

18. The title tells all in the notable, perhaps notorious, revolutionary tract, Bill Owens, *Lifting the Fog of War*, New York: Farrow, Straus, Giroux, 2000.

19. The best discussion by far is provided by the studies in Knox and Murray, eds., *The Dynamics of Military Revolution, 1300-2050.*

20. Hundley, *Past Revolutions, Future Transformations*, p. 27.

21. Colin S. Gray: *Weapons for Strategic Effect: How Important is Technology?* Occasional Paper 22, Maxwell AFB, AL: Air War College, Center for Strategy and Technology, January 2001; *Strategy for Chaos*.

22. Clausewitz, p. 566.

23. Not infrequently, a technological shortfall creates a demand for a supply of heroes. Such a supply can be easily exhausted.

24. Colin S. Gray, *Transformation and Strategic Surprise*, Carlisle, PA: Strategic Studies Institute, U.S. Army War College, April 2005.

25. See Bruce I. Gudmundsson, *Stormtroop Tactics: Innovation in the German Army, 1914-1918*, New York: Praeger, 1989. This excellent book suffers a little from a case of teutophilia. The author is slightly baffled by the indisputable fact that the German Army lost the war. American admirers of German military prowess quite often can seem almost embarrassed to have to concede, en passant, that, by the way, the superior military team lost!

26. The story is well told in Williamson Murray, "May 1940: Contingency and Fragility of the German RMA," in Knox and Murray, eds., *The Dynamics of Military Revolution, 1300-2050*, pp. 154-74. Robert Allan Doughty, *The Breaking Point: Sedan and the Fall of France, 1940*, Hamden, CT: Archon Books, 1990, is classic.

27. Robert R. Jones, "Relearning Counterinsurgency Warfare," *Parameters*, Vol. XXXIV, No. 1. Spring 2004, pp. 16-28, offers a plausible message for today. Some highly relevant background is to be found in Andrew F. Krepinevich, *The Army and Vietnam*, Baltimore: Johns Hopkins University Press, 1986.

28. I developed this point in my article, "RMAs and the Dimensions of Strategy," *Joint Force Quarterly*, No. 17, Autumn/Winter 1997-98, pp. 50-54.

29. Clausewitz, p. 605.

30. *Ibid.*, p. 89.

31. A near perfect example were the Anglo-French wars of the very late 17th, 18th, and early 19th centuries, especially in their maritime dimension. It may be needless to add that the political, and hence strategic, contexts did vary significantly from war to war. Nonetheless, the challenge to English, then British, security posed by France was essentially stable for more than a century.

32. George W. Bush, *The National Security Strategy of the United States of America*, Washington, DC: The White House, September 2002, is amazingly forthright in its declaration of a U.S. intention to remain strategically preeminent.

33. Colin S. Gray, *The Sheriff: America's Defense of the New World Order*, Lexington, KY: University Press of Kentucky, 2004.

34. In a now quite famous purple passage in his book, *Paradise and Power: America and Europe in the New World Order*, London: Atlantic Books, 2003, pp. 36-37, Robert Kagan explained colorfully the strategic context for the global sheriff.

Americans are "cowboys," Europeans love to say. And there is truth in this. The United States does act as an international sheriff, self-appointed perhaps but widely welcomed nonetheless, trying to enforce some peace and justice in what Americans see as a lawless world where outlaws need to be deterred or destroyed, often through the muzzle of a gun. Europe, by this Wild West analogy, is more like the saloonkeeper. Outlaws shoot sheriffs, not saloonkeepers. In fact, from the saloonkeeper's point of view, the sheriff trying to impose order by force can sometimes be more threatening than the outlaws, who may just want a drink.

35. See Qiao Liang and Wang Xiangsui, *Unrestricted Warfare: Assumptions on War and Tactics in the Age of Globalization*, Foreign Broadcast Information Service (FBIS) trans., Beijing: PLA Literature Arts Publishing House, February 1999.

36. A well-regarded short paper on "The Current Revolution in the Nature of Conflict" (July 2005), prepared by Chris Donnelly at Britain's Defence Academy for the attention of the Secretary of Defence, has this to say: "[W]e think of them [revolutions in the nature of conflict] as 'military events'. But in fact the principal drivers tend to be economic, social or political rather than military-technical. They are not just revolutions in the nature of battle." P. 1.

37. First-rate studies of military innovation in the interwar years, both its execution and its detection, monitoring, and comprehension, include Ernest May, ed., *Knowing One's Enemies: Intelligence Assessment before the Two World Wars*, Princeton, NJ: Princeton University Press, 1984; Wesley K. Wark, *The Ultimate Enemy: British Intelligence and Nazi Germany, 1933-1939*, Ithaca, NY: Cornell University Press, 1985; Murray and. Millett, eds., *Military Innovation in the Interwar Period*; Harold R. Winton and David R. Mets, eds., *The Challenge of Change: Military Institutions and New Realities, 1918-1941*, Lincoln, NE: University of Nebraska Press, 2000; Thomas G. Mahnken, *Uncovering Ways of War: US Intelligence and Foreign Military Innovation, 1918-1941*, Ithaca, NY: Cornell University Press, 2002; and John Ferris, *Intelligence and Strategy: Selected Essays*, London: Routledge, 2005, ch. 3, "Image and Accident: Intelligence and the Origins of the Second World War."

38. The authoritative, even quasi-official, German history of World War II is unambiguous in its judgment on the implications of Hitler's frank outlining of his plans for expansion to the country's military and diplomatic leaders on November 5, 1937. "From this point onwards, Hitler was not pursuing a policy at the risk of war, but a war policy, which he had thought out in advance and had been preparing since 1933." Wilhelm Deist, *et al.*, *Germany and the Second World War: Volume I, the Build-up of German Aggression*, Oxford: Clarendon Press, 2000, p. 638.

39. The Rimland concept was developed in the early 1940s by the Yale-based Dutch-American political scientist, Nicholas J. Spykman. See his books: *America's Strategy in World Politics: The United States and the Balance of Power*, New York: Harcourt, Brace, 1942; and *The Geography of the Peace, 1944*, Hamden, CT: Archon Books, 1969.

40. Clausewitz, p. 610.

41. This concern of mine is shared by Hew Strachan in his important article, "The Lost Meaning of Strategy," *Survival*, Vol. 47, No. 3, Autumn 2005, pp. 33-54.

42. Clausewitz, p. 183.

43. *Ibid.*

44. See Peter J. Schoomaker, *2004 Army Transformation Roadmap*, Washington, DC: Department of the Army, July 2004.

45. See Donald H. Rumsfeld, *Transformation Planning Guidance*, Washington, DC: Department of Defense, April 2003.

46. "The thesis of this book is clear—but as yet little understood: the way we make war reflects the way we make wealth . . ." Alvin and Heidi Toffler, *War and Anti-War: Survival at the Dawn of the 21st Century*, Boston: Little, Brown, 1993, p. 3.

47. See Rohan Gunaratna, *Inside Al Qaeda: Global Network of Terror*, New York: Columbia University Press, 2002; and Steve Coll, *Ghost Wars: the Secret History of the CIA, Afghanistan, and bin Laden, from the Soviet Invasion to September 10, 2001*, London: Penguin Books, 2004. The historical context is brilliantly explained from a viewpoint rarely considered seriously by Westerners, in M. J. Akbar, *The Shade of Swords: Jihad and the Conflict between Islam and Christianity*, London: Routledge, 2002.

48. Of recent years, there has been a revival of interest in the power of ideas to shape minds, societies, policy, and the course of history. An exemplar of this trend is Michael Burleigh, *The Third Reich: A New History*, London: Macmillan, 2000, which presents nazism as a political religion.

49. Edward N. Luttwak, "Toward Post-Heroic Warfare," *Foreign Affairs*, Vol. 74, No. 3, May/June 1995, pp. 109-122.

50. Although I advise careful study of warfare's social-cultural context, I must admit to a certain unease. It is some small comfort to note that other scholars, Richard K. Betts and Hew Strachan, have flagged the same disquiet. Specifically, it is possible to become so enamored of the possible significance of social and cultural factors, among many others, that one's strategic analysis ceases to be very strategic. In short, one may drown in context. A good idea, that context is vitally significant, becomes a bad idea if it promotes so much extra-strategic study that strategic analysis all but disappears. Given the long-standing strategy deficit which has plagued American performance in war, the last thing one wishes to encourage is any further dilution of that essential focus. Strategic studies become security studies, and security studies potentially include just about everything, a condition which Strachan rightly condemns thus: "by being inclusive [security studies] they end up by being nothing." "The Lost Meaning of Strategy," p. 47. Also, see Betts, "Should Strategic Studies Survive?" *World Politics*, Vol. 50, No. 1, October 1997, p. 27.

51. Paul Kennedy, *The Rise and Fall of the Great Powers: Economic Change and Military Conflict from 1500 to 2000*, New York: Random House, 1987. Kennedy's main argument is to the effect that military greatness imposes such an enervating

economic burden that it proves unsustainable. It carries the economic seeds of its own future destruction, always provided rival states do not write finis to the imperial story in the nearer term.

52. The clearest and most persuasive analysis is Murray and Knox, "Thinking About Revolutions in Military Affairs."

53. Stephen Biddle, *Afghanistan and the Future of Warfare: Implications for Army and Defense Policy*, Carlisle, PA: Strategic Studies Institute, U.S. Army War College, November 2002. Also see Stepehn Biddle, *Military Power: Explaining Victory and Defeat in Modern Battle*, Princeton, NJ: Princeton University Press, 2004, especially pp. 37-38.

54. British scientist, Martin Rees, advises that although "[t]here are physical limits to how finely silicon microchips can be etched by present techniques . . . new methods are already being developed that can print circuits on a much finer scale, so 'Moore's Law' need not level off." Rees proceeds to speculate that "quite different techniques — tiny crisscrossing optical beams, not involving chip circuits at all — may increase computing power still further." *Our Final Century: Will Civilization Survive the Twenty-First Century?* London: Arrow Books, 2003, p. 16.

55. See Murray and Millett, eds., *Military Innovation in the Interwar Period*; and Thomas G. Mahnken, "Beyond Blitzkrieg: Allied Responses to Combined Arms Armored Warfare during World War II," in Emily O. Goldman and Leslie C. Eliason, eds., *The Diffusion of Military Technology and Ideas*, Stanford, CA: Stanford University Press, pp. 243-266.

56. In support of this claim I cite the now well-known fact that for 40 years there were major difference between U.S. and Soviet approaches to nuclear strategy. Those differences were not, as many Americans believed in the 1960s and 1970s, the result of Soviet strategic intellectual backwardness, neither did they simply reflect distinctive paths in weapons choices driven by respective technological prowess. Instead, U.S. and Soviet strategies for nuclear weapons, and their motives and proposals for strategic arms limitation, were the product mainly of distinguishably different strategic and military cultures. This author was a participant observer of this long running controversy for 15 years or more. See Colin S. Gray, *Nuclear Strategy and National Style*, Lanham, MD: Hamilton Press, 1986.

57. A fine set of studies on the diffusion of technology and ideas concludes with the important judgment that,

> An innovation developed and honed in one setting is rarely transplanted wholly to another without modification. Historically, states have either adapted innovations to make them functionally effective in their new setting, or selected certain aspects of the model to adopt. Few chapters identify instances of faithful emulation. Departure from original patterns occur because the environment and values in the importing society usually diverge from those of the source.

Emily O. Goldman and Andrew L. Ross, "Conclusion: the Diffusion of Military

Technology and Ideas — Theory and Practice, Goldman and Eliason, eds., *The Diffusion of Military Technology and Ideas*, p. 386.

58. David J. Lonsdale, *Alexander: Killer of Men. Alexander the Great and the Macedonian Art of War*, London: Constable, 2005, p. 198.

59. *Ibid.*

60. Martin C. Libicki, "The Emerging Primacy of Information," *Orbis*, Vol. 40, No. 2, Spring 1996, pp. 261-274.

61. Bruce Berkowitz, *The New Face of War: How War Will Be Fought in the 21st Century*, New York: Free Press, 2003, p. 179.

62. J. C. Wylie, *Military Strategy: A General Theory of Power Control*, Annapolis, MD: Naval Institute Press, 1989, p. 72 (emphasis in the original).

63. Brian W. Blouet, ed., *Global Geostrategy: Mackinder and the Defence of the West*, London: Frank Cass, 2005, is a helpful collection of essays that treats many of the key themes in geopolitics.

64. Colin S. Gray, "Inescapable Geography," in Gray and Geoffrey Sloan, eds., *Geopolitics, Geography and Strategy*, London: Frank Cass, 1999, pp. 161-177.

65. See Thomas A. Keaney and Eliot A. Cohen, *Revolution in Warfare? Air Power in the Persian Gulf*, Annapolis, MD: Naval Institute Press, 1995. This book is a revised version of the Summary volume of the *Gulf War Air Power Survey*, published in 1993.

66. Vincent, *History*, p. 9.

67. International Institute for Strategic Studies (IISS), *Strategic Survey 2004/5*, London: Routledge, May 2005, p. 25.

68. The anti-historical blast in *Strategic Survey* is more than a little reminiscent of the trouble that Bernard Brodie had, and complained about repeatedly, with his long-time colleagues at RAND in general, and in the U.S. defense community as a whole. See his somewhat personal, even ad hominem, critique of the prophets and practitioners of systems analysis in *War and Politics*, New York: Macmillan, 1973, ch. 10. Brodie is right, but the personal dimension to his argument obliges us to treat it with some caution.

69. Echevarria, "The Trouble with History," p. 80 (emphasis added).

70. Schoomaker, *2004 Army Transformation Roadmap*.

71. This maxim of eternal worth is well-presented in Williamson Murray and Mark Grimsley, "Introduction: On Strategy," in Murray, MacGregor Knox, and Alvin Bernstein, eds., *The Making of Strategy: Rulers, States and War*, Cambridge: Cambridge University Press, 1994, p. 22. The authors qualify the maxim brilliantly with an all too pertinent observation, "but few can discern what is possible."

72. The scholarly literature on this subject is of high quality and has much merit, even though, in my opinion, it tends to come to unsound conclusions and offers unreliable advice for policy and strategy. See Martin van Creveld, *The Transformation*

of War, New York: Free Press, 1991; John Keegan, *A History of Warfare*, London: Hutchinson, 1993; Mary Kaldor, *New and Old Wars: Organized Violence in a Global Era*, Cambridge: Polity Press, 1999; Colin McInnes, *Spectator-Sport War: The West and Contemporary Conflict*, Boulder, CO: Lynne Rienner Publishers, 2002; James C. Kurth, "Clausewitz and the Two Contemporary Military Revolutions: RMA and RAM," in Bradford A. Lee and Karl F. Walling, eds., *Strategic Logic and Political Rationality: Essays in Honor of Michael I. Handel*, London: Frank Cass, 2003, pp. 274-297; Christopher Coker, *Waging War Without Warriors? The Changing Culture of Military Conflict*, Boulder, CO: Lynne Rienner Publishers, 2002; Christopher Coker, *The Future of War: The Re-Enchantment of War in the Twenty-First Century*, Oxford: Blackwell Publishing, 2004; Herfried Münkler, *The New Wars*, Cambridge: Polity Press, 2005; and Isabelle Duyvesteyn and Jan Angstrom, eds., *Rethinking the Nature of War*, London: Frank Cass, 2005.

73. Chris Donnelly observes that "there is today an almost total lack of media correspondents and editors who really understand defence and security issues." "The Current Revolution in the Nature of Conflict," p. 4.

74. "But in terms of the history of warfare, the most significant point about the war with Iraq is perhaps that soldiers are accountable as in no other age for the war that they fight. Not just for winning the war, which is all that mattered in centuries past, but for every action that takes place on the battlefield." Eleanor Goldsworthy, "Warfare in Context," *The RUSI Journal*, Vol. 148, No. 3, June 2003, p. 19.

75. See the timely, well-argued, but dangerously enticing article, Robert H. Scales, Jr., "Culture-Centric Warfare," U.S. Naval Institute *Proceedings*, Vol. 130, No. 10, October 2004, pp. 32-36.

76. Murray and Knox, "Conclusion: The Future Behind Us," in Knox and Murray, eds., *The Dynamics of Military Revolution, 1300-2050*, p. 192 ff.

77. For a superior recent manifestation of fairly deadly combat between historians, see: "Military Revolutions: A Forum," *Historically Speaking*, Vol. IV, No. 4, April 2003, pp. 2-14. The contributors to this internecine bloodletting were Geoffrey Parker and Jeremy Black, the primary champions, with commentaries also by Dennis Showalter, sensible as always, Jeffrey Clarke from the Army, who was noncombative, concluding with an unrepentant blast by Parker. On balance, it must be said that Black won the debate. Parker overplayed and oversimplified his argument in favor of there having been a technology driven Military Revolution from 1530 to 1660. However, the process of debate did cause an escalation of extremism in the exchanges.

78. Especially Murray and Millett, eds., *Military Innovation in the Interwar Period*. And one should not forget the monumental three-volume study of comparative military effectiveness led by these authors in the mid to late 1980s, also with the sponsorship of Marshall's Office of Net Assessment. See Allan R. Millett and Williamson Murray, eds., *Military Effectiveness: Vol. I, The First World War; Vol. II, The Interwar Period; Vol. III, The Second World War*, Boston: Allen and Unwin, 1988.

These outstanding books have much to say that is relevant to the understanding of revolutionary change in warfare. There is no denying, though, that they do suffer noticeably from some important conceptual shortfalls. There is a pervasive theory shortfall which most plausibly is attributable to the fact that the project was conducted almost entirely by professional historians, without the conceptual discipline from social science that it needed.

79. Murray and Knox, "Conclusion: The Future Behind Us," pp. 192-193 (emphasis in the original).

80. Michael Howard is quoted informally in Echevarria, "The Trouble with History," p. 89, n. 14.

81. Unfortunately for the theorist who relies heavily on the "evidence" of the past, history is almost maliciously well-endowed with inconvenient exceptions to favored postulates, theories, and meta-narratives. As Napoleon said, "[t]here is no authority without exception . . ." Napoleon, *The Military Maxims of Napoleon*, David G. Chandler trans., New York: Macmillan, 1988, p. 70, "Maxim XLII."

82. For the industrial points, see Guido Knapp's study of Admiral Wilhelm Canaris, Head of the *Abwehr*, in his book, *Hitler's Warriors*, Stroud, UK: Sutton Publishing, 2005, esp. p. 324. General Lieutenant Friedrich Paulus, the chief planner for Barbarossa with his appointment to be senior Quartermaster on the Army General Staff, was not seriously troubled by doubts about the quality of the intelligence on which he based his planning, any more than he was by doubts about the logistical feasibility of the campaign. *Ibid.*, pp. 200-202. Political and strategic assumptions dominated the analysis. Since the campaign, which is to say the war, was confidently expected to destroy the fielded Red Army close to the recently advanced frontiers of the Soviet Union, and because the entire venture was calculated to last little more than 6 weeks, perhaps 2 to 3 months, what did it matter how many additional divisions the enemy might raise, or how many tanks his factories could produce? For the statistics cited in the text on the Soviet and NKVD divisional order of battle, for the Red Army see Horst Boog, *et al.*, *Germany and the Second World War: Volume IV, The Attack on the Soviet Union*, Oxford: Clarendon Press, 1998, pp. 320-325; while for the NKVD see Glantz, *Colossus Reborn*, ch. 5.

83. Antulio J. Echevarria II, *After Clausewitz: German Military Thinkers Before the Great War*, Lawrence, KS: University Press of Kansas, 2000. Also see Niall Ferguson, *The Pity of War*, London: Allen Lane, 1998, p. 101; and especially Hew Strachan, *The First World War: Volume I, To Arms*, Oxford: Oxford University Press, 2001, pp. 98-99. Although military leaders almost everywhere expected a lengthy conflict in military terms, they were assured by civilian economic experts that this could not happen because a general war must precipitate a no less general financial collapse which would render further hostilities impossible. This was a significant illusion prior to 1914.

84. These are not uncontested judgments. See: Stephen Peter Rosen, "Military Effectiveness: Why Society Matters," *International Security*, Vol. 19, No. 4, Spring 1995, pp. 5-31; and for a more skeptical view, Michael C. Desch, "Culture Clash: Assessing the Importance of Ideas in Security Studies," *International Security*, Vol.

23, No. 1, Summer 1998, pp. 141-170; a recent scholarly work offers an interesting collection of focused comparative case studies of six countries: India, Nigeria, Japan, Australia, Russia, and Germany. John Glenn, Darryl Howlett, and Stuart Poore, eds., *Neorealism Versus Strategic Culture*, Burlington, VT: Ashgate Publishing, 2004.

85. Mahnken, *Uncovering Ways of War.*

86. Black, *Rethinking Military History*, pp. 13-22.

87. Mahnken, *Uncovering Ways of War*, pp. 179-180.

88. Clausewitz, p. 89.

89. John Keegan, *The Iraq War*, London: Hutchinson, 2004, p. 6.

90. I am grateful to Dr. Antulio Echevarria of the Army War College, Strategic Studies Institute, for assisting my Clausewitzian education by emphasizing to me the extent of the potential differences of relative influence among the trinitarian elements. He is right, but his valid point does not dissuade me from insisting upon the overall authority of Clausewitz's absolute claim that "all wars are things of the *same* nature." Clausewitz, p. 606.

91. With reference to airpower, examples of the potential for the strategically confusing influence of a radical change in warfare include the German development of an unduly short-range air force, one much hampered additionally by many unsound operational and technical choices. The defects of the *Luffwaffte* may well have cost Germany the war. Also, the United States pursued its all-geographies nuclear revolution in the 1950s and 1960s with such dedication that the armed forces were desperately short of effective close ground support aircraft in Vietnam, a role partially filled by the invention of the helicopter gunship. In addition, in the 1960s the U.S. military discovered that its prospective excellence in the delivery of nuclear ordnance in Europe had not equipped it well to conduct old fashioned dog-fights. There was a need for fighters to have guns as well as bomb racks and rockets. The subsequent development of the loved and hated A-10 *Warthog*, was a reluctant recognition by the Air Force that it had no choice but to share the glory in some wars with the army.

92. Gray, *Strategy for Chaos*, esp. pp. 274-275.

93. Lonsdale, *Alexander: Killer of Men*, p. 230. My argument is heavily indebted to this excellent work. Also, I am grateful to Dr. Lonsdale for his patient and enthusiastic efforts to explain just why Alexander merits billing as the finest strategist in history. I was convinced, a judgment I have not sought to conceal in the text. Not even awful movies can seriously dent his popular reputation, though they can threaten to do so.

94. See Michael C. C. Adams, *Fighting for Defeat: Union Military Failure in the East, 1861-1865*, Lincoln, NE: University of Nebraska Press, 1992.

95. This incontrovertible claim is illustrated forbiddingly by a diagram in my *Strategy for Chaos*, p. 126, Figure 5.2: "The 17 Dimensions of Strategy." This diagram may have lost me some of my less tolerant readers.

96. A terse presentation of these lists is offered as Figure 5.1, *Ibid.*, p. 123, "The Elements/Dimensions of Strategy: Three Cuts."

97. See my chapter, "The American Way of War: Critique and Implications" in Anthony McIvor, ed., *Rethinking the Principles of War: The Future of Warfare*, Annapolis, MD: Naval Institute Press, 2005, pp. 13-40.

98. Clausewitz, p. 75 (emphasis in the original).

99. Gray, *Strategy for Chaos*, ch. 3, "RMA Dynamics."

100. See Keith B. Payne, *The Fallacies of Cold War Deterrence and a New Direction*, Lexington: University Press of Kentucky, 2001; while Colin S. Gray, *The Second Nuclear Age*, Boulder, CO: Lynne Reinner Publishers, 1999, explains the proposition of two nuclear ages.

101. This is the utterly convincing overall conclusion to the superior studies collected in Goldman and Eliason, eds., *The Diffusion of Military Technology and Ideas*.

102. Murray and Knox, "Conclusion: The Future Before Us," p. 193.

103. *Ibid.*, p. 185.

www.ingramcontent.com/pod-product-compliance
Lightning Source LLC
Chambersburg PA
CBHW080538290526
45790CB00006B/2464